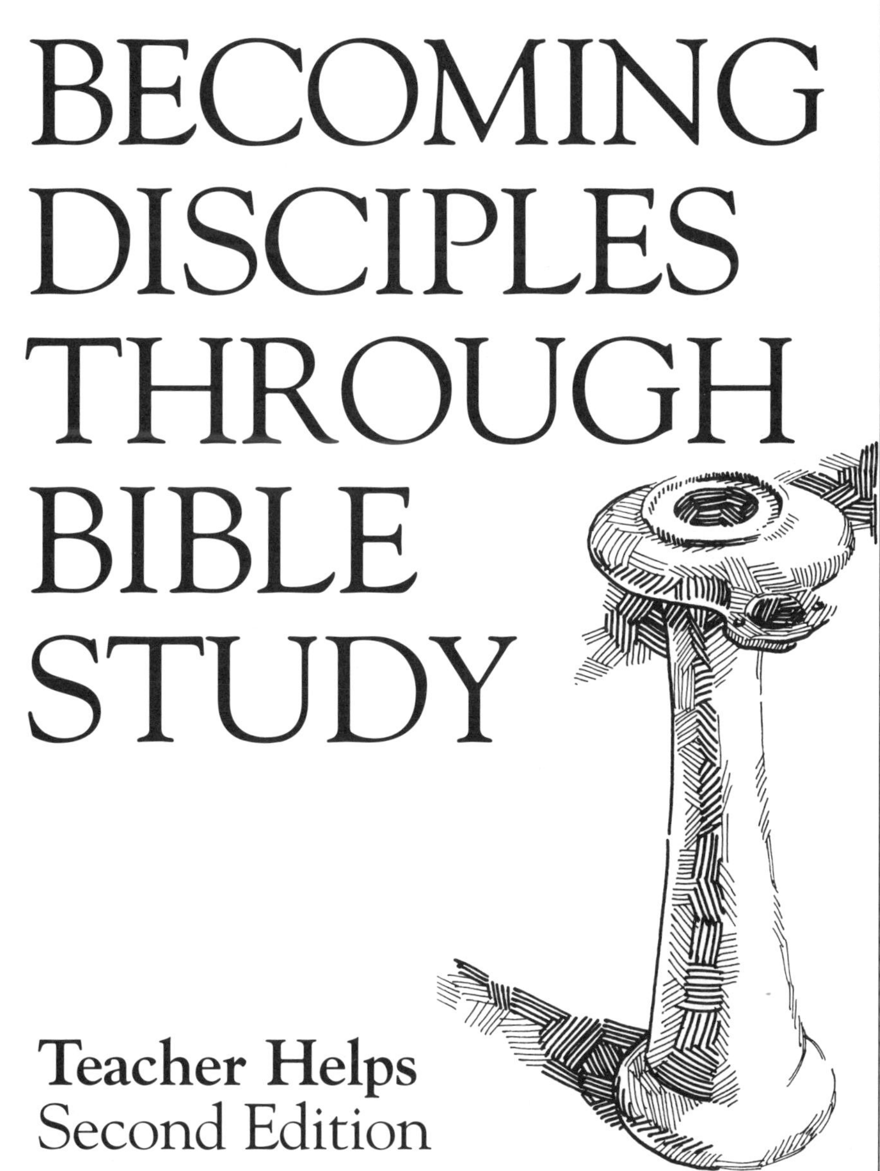

BECOMING DISCIPLES THROUGH BIBLE STUDY

Teacher Helps
Second Edition

DISCIPLE: BECOMING DISCIPLES THROUGH BIBLE STUDY
Teacher Helps

Harriett Jane Olson, Editorial Director, Abingdon Press; Mark Price, Senior Editor; Cindy Caldwell, Development Editor; Kent Sneed, Design Manager.

05 06 07 08 09 10 11 12 13 14 — 10 9 8 7 6 5 4 3 2

Contents

Put the Study Manual to Work

Each part of the study manual has a specific function both in daily preparation and in the weekly group meeting.

Theme Word

The theme word gives a clue to the subject of the lesson and the Scripture being studied in the lesson.

- Display the word during each group meeting.
- Suggest that persons memorize the theme word along with the lesson title to help them recall the sequence and content of the biblical story.

Theme Verse

The theme verse(s) expresses the focus of the lesson and might be read or recited from memory during the opening moment of devotion.

Title

The titles are descriptive of events or content, and together they summarize the biblical story from Creation to Revelation.

Our Human Condition

"Our Human Condition" is a statement of *who we are*. The "Marks of Discipleship" are statements of *whom we are committing ourselves to become,* and as such, suggest a resolution to "Our Human Condition." Encourage persons to restate "Our Human Condition" in terms of their own experience.

Assignment

Scripture is central to DISCIPLE, and the gaining and maintaining of the discipline of daily reading and study of Scripture are essential to the process of becoming disciples.

- The "Assignment" section indicates when to read the week's Scripture and when to read the study manual and write the responses called for.
- Insist on daily notetaking along with daily Scripture reading. The second page of each lesson in the manual provides space. The main purpose for taking notes is to have a personal record of information gleaned from Scripture and of insights and questions about the Scripture. Many activities will call for use of the notes in group discussion and interaction.
- Ask group members to covenant together to prepare this weekly page of notes.
- Challenge group members through your own example of daily reading, study, and notetaking.
- Encourage persons to mark their Bibles as they read. (See "Marking Your Bible," page 7.)
- Make use of the work persons have done during the week. The extent to which you recognize and use the preparation group members have made will determine the degree of commitment they continue to bring to completing assignments.

Prayer

The prayer psalm printed in the manual is a starting point for personal prayer.

- Encourage persons to jot down concerns about which they want to pray during the week and to add concerns from their daily study of Scripture.
- Establish a plan for group members to pray for one another. Each week write persons' names on slips of paper for exchange at the group meeting so that each group member will have the name of one other person to pray for daily.

The Bible Teaching

This section comments on the Scripture and draws meaning from it.

- Write notes in the margin as you read and during discussion in the group meeting while others are telling what they have learned.
- Decide how you will use the information persons write in the blanks in this section. Some information will be suited to response on a voluntary basis, in pairs or in threes; other information might be discussed in the entire group.

Marks of Discipleship

The marks of discipleship summarize major characteristics of the disciple of Jesus Christ and emphasize the practice of discipleship.

- Make the connection between "Marks of Discipleship" and "Our Human Condition."
- Vary the approaches you use for having persons talk about their written responses in this section.
- In instances that call for practicing discipleship in a specific way, decide as a group how to proceed.

If You Want to Know More

This section provides practice in using reference materials and in presenting information.

- Make use of the initiative of group members by providing time for them to report their individual research and study.
- Scan the information in this section. Some of it is useful at more than one point in the study.

Weekly Group Schedule and Procedure

Teacher helps for each of the thirty-four group meetings (pages 16–50) follow this format. Copy the planning sheet on page 6 to use in preparing your weekly group meeting plan. ***NOTE:*** *This resource has been revised to make use of the Revised 2005 set of video segments. Check the front of your VHS or DVD case for the Revised 2005 banner displayed on the lower right corner. If there is no banner on the case, turn to page 51 for information about using the Second Edition (1993) Video Segments.*

GATHERING AND PRAYER

(5 minutes)
Begin on time with those who are there. A moment of worship could include the theme word, theme verse, "Our Human Condition," and daily prayer from the study manual.

VIDEO SEGMENT

(20 minutes)
The video segment will provide persons a common body of information to which to react and will focus attention on the subject of the group meeting.

Teacher helps for each lesson

- suggest a way to prepare group members to view the video segment;
- provide a summary of the ideas in the segment;
- suggest one way the group may respond to what they have heard.

Encourage notetaking during the viewing.

Occasionally the group may want to view a video segment a second time to gain fuller understanding.

Preview the video segment. Prepare some questions to help group members make connections between the video content and what they have read in the Bible and in the study manual.

SCRIPTURE AND STUDY MANUAL

(50 minutes)
Much of the discussion and activity during this time will result from the reading and study persons have done and from their notes and questions.

Because you will be dealing with large amounts of Scripture and commentary on the Scripture, plan some procedures that help persons identify, clarify, organize, and master information they have gathered in their study. Plan some procedures that take persons beyond information to meaning.

Guard against repeating in the group meeting what persons have already done in their preparation.

As you prepare to guide this part of the meeting, put yourself in the place of the group members and ask yourself what kind of activities would allow you to make use of your preparation.

BREAK

(10 minutes)
Stay with the allotted time. Limit refreshments.

ENCOUNTER THE WORD

(40 minutes)
This time focuses on group study of a passage selected from the assigned Scripture. Group members will have read the passage but will not have studied it in detail. No mention of this activity is made in the study manual, and group members will not know before the meeting what passage they will be studying together.

Teacher helps for each lesson indicate the passage selected for study and one or more study approaches. The approaches are described in detail in *Teaching the Bible to Adults and Youth,* by Dick Murray (Abingdon Press, 1993).

- Familiarize yourself with the suggested approach.
- Test the approach with the selected passage.
- Identify clearly the steps you will follow in guiding the study.

MARKS OF DISCIPLESHIP

(20 minutes)
At this point in the group meeting, you will consider what it means to be a disciple. Draw on the work persons have done in this section of the study manual and on group study and discussion.

The mark of discipleship for each lesson is stated in both the study manual and the teacher helps. Teacher helps emphasize the importance of making the connection between the mark of discipleship and "Our Human Condition" stated at the beginning of the lesson.

Becoming disciples is the point of this section and the point of DISCIPLE. Therefore, exercise careful control of time throughout the group meeting in order to have the time necessary for this section.

CLOSING AND PRAYER

(5 minutes)
Close the session on time with a prayer or song.

Group Meeting Plan

Lesson ______ Title ______________________________

GATHERING AND PRAYER

(5 minutes) (   )

VIDEO SEGMENT

(20 minutes) (   )
Presenter(s):

Prepare to View Video

View Video
Summary of video content:

Discuss After Viewing Video

SCRIPTURE AND STUDY MANUAL

(50 minutes) (   )

BREAK

(10 minutes) (   )

ENCOUNTER THE WORD

(40 minutes) (   )
Scripture selection:

MARKS OF DISCIPLESHIP

(20 minutes) (   )

CLOSING AND PRAYER

(5 minutes) (   )

Keep in Mind

MARKING YOUR BIBLE

Start DISCIPLE study with a fresh, unmarked Bible so that you approach the Scripture anew without the influence of earlier notations and markings.

Mark your Bible to turn it into a personalized study Bible.

- Use colored pencils or highlighters, different colors to indicate different kinds of information or reasons for marking.
- Know why you are marking particular material.
  What you mark may differ from one type of biblical literature to another.
  You may want to mark words or phrases that give you clues to the writer's message, names of people and places, sequence in the action, verses that have special meaning for you.
- Resist the temptation to mark the familiar simply because it is familiar.
- Indicate new insights or points about which you have questions.
- Identify passages to memorize.

Discuss these ideas with other DISCIPLE group members and encourage them to mark their Bibles as they read the daily assignments.

RESOURCES FOR TEACHING

These resources are suggested especially for the teacher and are additional to those listed in the study manual.

Eerdmans Dictionary of the Bible, edited by David Noel Freedman (William B. Eerdman, 2000).

The Women's Bible Commentary, edited by Carol A. Newsom and Sharon H. Ringe (Westminster/ John Knox Press, 1992).

The Macmillan Bible Atlas (Third Edition), by Yohanan Aharoni and Michael Avi-Yonah; revised by Anson F. Rainey and Ze'ev Safrai (Macmillan Publishing Company, 1993).

Reading Scripture as the Word of God (Second Edition), by George Martin (Servant Books, 1975, 1982).

MEETING LOCATION AND EQUIPMENT

Consider the following factors in choosing and preparing a place for the weekly group meetings:

- physical accessibility to all group members;
- private enough to insure no interruptions;
- adequate space for sitting or standing in groups for study activities;
- appropriate, comfortable furniture, including tables large enough to allow spreading out books and writing;
- availability of childcare;
- appropriate heating and cooling;
- video equipment in good working order, placed for easy viewing;
- chalkboard or newsprint pad and adequate display area for maps and other visual aids.

SOCIAL OCCASIONS

Fellowship, trust, and caring will deepen as persons get to know one another at times and in situations other than the weekly group meeting.

- Plan occasions when members invite spouses, other family members, and friends for a time of relaxed visiting, playing, and eating together.
- You may want to celebrate holidays or days or events that are special to members of the group.
- The point of such gatherings is to have leisure time together for getting to know one another better. So keep the occasions informal and fairly simple.

SERVICE OF RECOGNITION

Completion of study of DISCIPLE by groups of twelve and their teacher is cause for recognition, celebration, and thanksgiving by the whole congregation. Plan such an occasion as a part of a regular morning or evening worship service.

- Invite a member of the administrative council or administrative board or another representative of the congregation to express the gratitude of the congregation to those who have studied and prepared themselves for further service as disciples in and through the congregation.
- Ask group members to describe what the study experience meant to them.
- Report decisions about the specific forms of discipleship persons have chosen for subsequent months.
- Include prayer for members of the congregation who will form similar groups of twelve for study and training in discipleship.
- Present certificates of recognition to persons who have completed DISCIPLE.

Marks of Discipleship

Each DISCIPLE *lesson identifies a particular mark of discipleship. All thirty-four marks are listed here.*

Disciples of Jesus Christ

1. place themselves under the power and authority of Scripture.
2. know they belong to God, that God has claim on them.
3. acknowledge their rebellion, accept responsibility for their sin, and repent.
4. respond to God's call to enter the covenant community of faith and express commitment to the covenant through the tithe.
5. hear and obey God's call to be bearers of God's message of deliverance.
6. keep God's law by doing it.
7. commit themselves to corporate worship.
8. provide a sense of direction and purpose through godly, obedient leadership.
9. maintain a perspective on leadership that supports and respects godly leaders but give true allegiance only to God.
10. recognize and listen to prophetic voices raised about community, nation, and world and at times become the prophetic voice.
11. accept consequences of their sin, seek forgiveness, look for healing and new opportunities for faithfulness.
12. choose to serve rather than to despair when suffering the consequences of sin.
13. trust God with all their thoughts and feelings.
14. strive to live in harmony with God's laws even though obedience is costly.
15. trust God in the face of unexplained suffering.
16. sense their unity with the historic people of God and live in hope with a vision of God's kingdom.
17. hear the gospel of Jesus Christ in the context of unity with the historic people of God.
18. accept Christ's call to radical discipleship.
19. abandon sham and pretense, become vulnerable, and enter the ministry of making disciples.
20. understand their ministry as a call to self-denial and suffering.
21. throw their weight with God's mission to the least, the last, the lost.
22. experience life in Jesus Christ.
23. sense the inner assurance of abundant, eternal life.
24. experience the presence and the power of the Holy Spirit in their life.
25. witness to others in order to lead them to Jesus Christ.
26. receive and trust the forgiving love of God in Jesus Christ and serve out of love and gratitude.
27. love.
28. experience and express freedom as loving God and loving neighbor.
29. seek sound teaching under the guidance of faithful leaders.
30. accept God's forgiveness.
31. know themselves as distinctive, peculiar people bearing the inner mark of character and the outer mark of compassion.
32. remain faithful to God in the midst of persecution and suffering.
33. use their gifts in ministry to others.
34. commit their life completely to God to serve as God wills.

Preparing to Teach DISCIPLE

- Prepare as a participant in the group, a learner among learners, as well as the teacher of the group.

- Do not rely on your familiarity with Scripture or on study done previously. Come to each lesson and its daily assignments as a beginner, as though you were reading the Scripture passages for the first time.

- Expect weekly preparation by group members and plan the group meeting process on that basis.

- Your role in the group meeting will be mainly in keeping the process going rather than in being the giver of information. No doubt, members of the group will look to you for some new or additional information, but don't let them put you into the position of being the authority or the expert. Regularly change where you sit in the group to avoid authority being given to one person in one place.

- Pay attention to the amount of time available for covering the main parts of the work to be done in each group meeting: use of the video segment, review and discussion of the weekly assignment, group study of a passage of Scripture, and commitment to ministry.

- Plan activities that will allow a balance among work done in the total group, work done in small groups or pairs, and work done as individuals. Choice of activity or teaching approach will vary according to the particular Scripture being studied.

- Your own reading of the assigned Scripture and the study manual will suggest to you ways of reviewing and making use of the material in the group meeting.

- Decide a sequence and process for handling the daily study notes persons have written. Here are some possibilities:

  1. Work through the sheet of notes and related Scriptures day by day, talking together in the total group, in small groups, or in pairs.

  2. Identify and list on newsprint all the questions persons had as they did their reading and study in preparation for the group meeting. Some of these questions will be answered by group members; others may require further study and discussion by the group.

  3. Work together to identify and organize the information gathered by group members in their study:
     - → Make time charts;
     - → develop glossaries of words;
     - → list key persons and events;
     - → identify and discuss biblical and theological ideas;
     - → establish the setting of the Scriptures being studied;
     - → make connections to other Scriptures and to life situations;
     - → discuss insights, experiences, feelings.

  4. Interpret the text in terms of the meaning originally intended.

- Anticipate the points where the group might get sidetracked or take a direction different from the one you have planned: the raising of an unanswerable question or a theological issue over which differences of opinion or debate are likely to occur. Be prepared to handle such occurrences.

- Include time in your plan for hearing reports from group members who have done additional study and research. If several persons have prepared reports on the same subject, vary the presentation through the use of a panel, by having one person give the report and others provide additional details, or form small groups for hearing the reports.

- Try to have some activity in each group meeting that has the group reading Scripture aloud or hearing the Scriptures read aloud.

- Plan an occasional activity that will require group members to use Bible commentaries, atlases, and dictionaries during the meeting to do further research for clarification or to locate additional information.

Group Building and Maintenance

The Climate for a Good Group

A good climate for study may be described in words such as these: *warmth, trust, enthusiasm, patience, open-mindedness, caring, acceptance, sensitivity, humor,* and *informality.*

In a healthy study climate, both the individual and the group are respected. Persons are attentive and sensitive to one another's thoughts and feelings, and persons feel comfortable in expressing honestly their deepest thoughts and feelings.

Drawing Out Quiet Persons

- Recognize that persons participate in ways other than talking and that a person has a right not to speak. Allow persons to pass rather than respond to a particular question or in a particular activity.
- Emphasize that all contributions have value. Hesitancy to speak may be related to a fear of saying the wrong thing or of appearing foolish.
- Be sensitive to when the quiet person may want to speak and simply needs some encouragement from the teacher. Watch for nonverbal clues. Take care not to embarrass by asking a direct question but rather by inviting a person to speak through such phrases as "You look as though you would like to add something."
- Plan small group discussion and activity, because those who are reluctant to participate in conversation in the larger group may feel comfortable doing so in a small group. Put groups together with care. Begin by putting the quieter persons together and the more dominant persons together. Gradually mix the groups so that persons will have opportunity to work with everyone.

Working With the Person Who Monopolizes

Tact and sensitivity are called for in responding to persons who tend to monopolize the conversation in the group.

- Be sensitive to what the persons are saying by their behavior as well as in their words.
- Recognize that your attitude toward the person who is dominating will be communicated through your tone of voice, body language, and facial expression as well as through your words.
- One response you may make is to summarize what the person has said and invite others to add to the discussion or to give their opinion.
- Lessen the opportunity for domination by a person or persons through the choice of group activities that employ small group work or team work or directed work that involves response from each person in turn.
- Rely on other group members to help manage the group process. When a group is functioning well, all persons in the group take some responsibility for participation and thereby cut down the possibility of one person dominating.

Group building and maintenance should be discussed when the study group is forming and deciding on ground rules. The ground rules might include some agreements about how persons are expected to participate and how the group will monitor itself.

Handling Conflicting Opinions in the Study Group

A healthy group climate depends on the understanding that differences of opinion are welcomed, that persons are encouraged to think for themselves, and that persons may feel comfortable in disagreeing with one another and with the teacher.

The teacher who is not personally threatened by views contrary to his or her own will quickly establish a tone of trust and acceptance in the group.

When conflict of opinion occurs, treat it as good, natural, and potentially rewarding.

- Maintain responsibility for the direction of the session.
- Keep the exchange of ideas focused on the topic, not on the persons involved in the discussion.
- At appropriate points in the discussion, summarize the major points and identify the points of difference and agreement.
- Continually relate the discussion to the session topic.
- Turn the discussion into an occasion for further work by the group through use of Bible dictionaries, commentaries, and other such aids.
- Recognize that sometimes resolution is not desirable, necessary, or possible, and that continuing difference of opinion is acceptable.
- If the discussion is not relevant to all group members, suggest that those who wish may talk further after the group has adjourned.
- Be aware of time and know when to move on with other work planned for the session.
- Compliment the group on the enthusiasm and strong feelings they bring to their discussion of such matters.
- Demonstrate caring and acceptance of persons both during and after points of conflict.

Preparing Questions and Leading Discussion

Group discussion that goes beyond the sharing of opinions or biases and superficial answers requires careful preparation by individual group members and by the teacher. Thinking that goes into productive discussion combines purpose and discipline.

PREPARING QUESTIONS

Be clear about what you want to accomplish through the questions you prepare.

- Questions can help persons think.
- Questions can open minds to new insights or knowledge.
- Questions can enable the examining of an idea, an understanding, an assumption.
- Questions often require probing deeper into a subject.

Different kinds of questions serve different purposes. Write questions with specific functions in mind.

- If your purpose is to gather or call to mind certain information, write questions that use recall, ask for facts, or require a specific correct answer.
- If your purpose is to organize data, write questions that ask persons to describe, compare, or contrast data.
- If your purpose is to analyze a situation or an action, write questions that call for explanation or reasons related to the situation or action.
- If your purpose is to make connections or draw conclusions, write questions that call for persons to summarize or state the relationship or connection among previously unrelated data.
- If your purpose is to have persons make judgments or evaluate, write questions that call for them to tell which choice is best according to specific criteria.
- If your purpose is to speculate about an outcome or a situation, write open-ended questions that allow for imagination and the identification of many possibilities.

Know what kind of question you are asking and indicate to the group the reason you are asking it.

When writing questions, keep these considerations in mind:

- Generally yes-and-no questions are too specific and tend to close off discussion.
- Questions are generally poor when their answer is too self-evident, when no answer is possible, when they are too involved, or when they are too vague.
- A good mixture of questions deals with information and with feelings and experiences.
- The best questions are stated simply and have only one focus.
- A good question generally takes persons back to earlier study and preparation and stimulates further inquiry.
- Key words for factual questions are *what, where, when, why, who,* and *how.*
- Before using the questions you have written to lead discussion, test the questions by trying to answer them yourself.

LEADING DISCUSSION

- State the question to be discussed. Help group members to know what they are discussing and why.
- Have in mind some idea of how the discussion ought to develop.
- Allow time for thought. Don't be afraid of silence, because silence need not be empty; and it invites thought. Don't rush to rephrase the question. If the question is well written, it will bring response eventually. Avoid answering your own questions, because persons will soon learn that you do and will depend on you to do so.
- Listen. Be sensitive to feelings as well as to words. Listening includes awareness of the speaker's point of view as well as the words being heard. Occasionally summarize what is being said without evaluating or judging.
- Indicate your listening by eye contact, a nod of the head, and a spoken word or two.
- Remember that you stop listening when you begin to think about how you are going to respond.
- Avoid approving or disapproving, agreeing or disagreeing (unless there is an error in fact) with what a person is saying.
- Acceptance of people does not require acceptance of their ideas, interpretations, attitudes.
- Create possibilities for all persons to contribute so that none monopolizes the discussion.
- Know where you are headed with the discussion so that as other questions arise you will not lose the direction you first set.

Principles for Bible Study

1. The Word of God is Jesus Christ, and the words of the Bible tell us about that Word. Therefore, when we study the words of the Bible we always look behind, in, and through those words for God's Word—Jesus Christ.

2. No Christian has a monopoly on understanding either God's Word or the words of the Scripture. This includes biblical scholars and the most unlearned Christian. All of us must listen to one another as we seek to understand the richness of God's gifts.

3. We must assume everyone has Christian integrity and not accuse one another of being unchristian, no matter how unusual are the opinions.

4. We must further assume that we will arrive at different understandings of portions of Scripture and that that will not disturb God as much as it will some of us.

5. Few of us will know Hebrew or Greek, and we therefore need to use a variety of English versions to try to understand the text.

6. While we accept our differences, we do not feel that those differences are unimportant, or that they should be ignored or treated as if they did not matter.

7. Different biblical understandings can remain among us, but we can still be warm Christian friends. In fact, as we grow to better understand our differences, we can grow in our appreciation of one another.

Orientation Meeting

When you have the full list of persons who have made the commitment to be a part of your DISCIPLE group, schedule a one-to-one-and-a-half-hour orientation meeting one week prior to the first weekly group meeting.

The purpose of the orientation meeting is

- to discuss and agree on a schedule for the nine-month study;
- to distribute the study manuals and become acquainted with the lesson format;
- to understand the commitment that is being undertaken by members of the group.

Explain the small-group process you will be using and emphasize that you are a learner among learners, not a lecturer or information giver, and that you will be an equal participant in the activities.

Describe the environment for study as one of openness and trust where every person's opinions will be valued.

Emphasize that as the study goes forward and the bond among group members deepens, confidentiality will be an important factor; and that if a situation arises when you cannot be present to lead a session, you will ask members of the group to lead the session, not someone from outside the group.

Emphasize that you will be paying close attention to time during the weekly meeting and that all parts of the group meeting format will be covered every week.

Stress that you will start the weekly group meeting on time and end on time.

Explain that during Session 33 group members will be making decisions about their discipleship commitment for the months ahead. That session works well in a retreat setting. You may want to tentatively schedule a retreat.

Mention the hope that from the group will come persons who will train for and teach DISCIPLE.

Don't assume that all persons will know how to use the aids in their Bibles. Plan some practice in reading footnotes, looking at maps and charts, using cross-references in the Bible, and in discovering information in general articles and introductory pages to the Bible.

Identify additional sources of information: Bible dictionaries, atlases, commentaries, and concordances. Let persons know if the church has such sources available and how they might borrow them.

Distribute during the meeting the thirty-four-week schedule, study manuals, handbooks, and "Principles for Bible Study."

Orientation Meeting Agenda

7:00 P.M. Prayer

7:05 P.M. Group member introductions.

7:10 P.M. Verify the meeting calendar.
- Discuss holiday breaks.
- Make necessary adjustments.

7:20 P.M. Preview the study manual and how it will be used (see study manual, page 4 and teacher helps, page 4).
- Explain the need for a good study Bible.
- Emphasize daily notetaking.

7:35 P.M. Review the weekly meeting schedule and format (see teacher helps, page 5).
- Discuss related issues—meeting location, video setup, childcare arrangements, refreshment schedule.
- Mention the significance and scheduling of Session 33.

7:50 P.M. Read "Principles for Bible Study" responsively.
- Highlight transformation as the key to DISCIPLE.

7:55 P.M. Emphasize congregational support and mention the service of recognition to be planned (see handbook, page 23).

8:00 P.M. Preview Session 1.
- Highlight daily assignments.
- Establish a plan of mutual prayer support.

8:10 P.M. Explore study aids in the Bible.
- Identify additional sources of information.

8:25 P.M. Closing Covenant
Reiterate the commitment required of DISCIPLE Bible Study (see handbook, pages 18–19).
Lead group in covenanting together to
- Pray daily for each other.
- Prepare daily by reading and taking notes.
- Be present every week but faithful to study when absent.
- Participate in every session by both listening and discussing.
- Commit to discipleship.

8:30 P.M. Dismiss

Notes

DISCIPLE

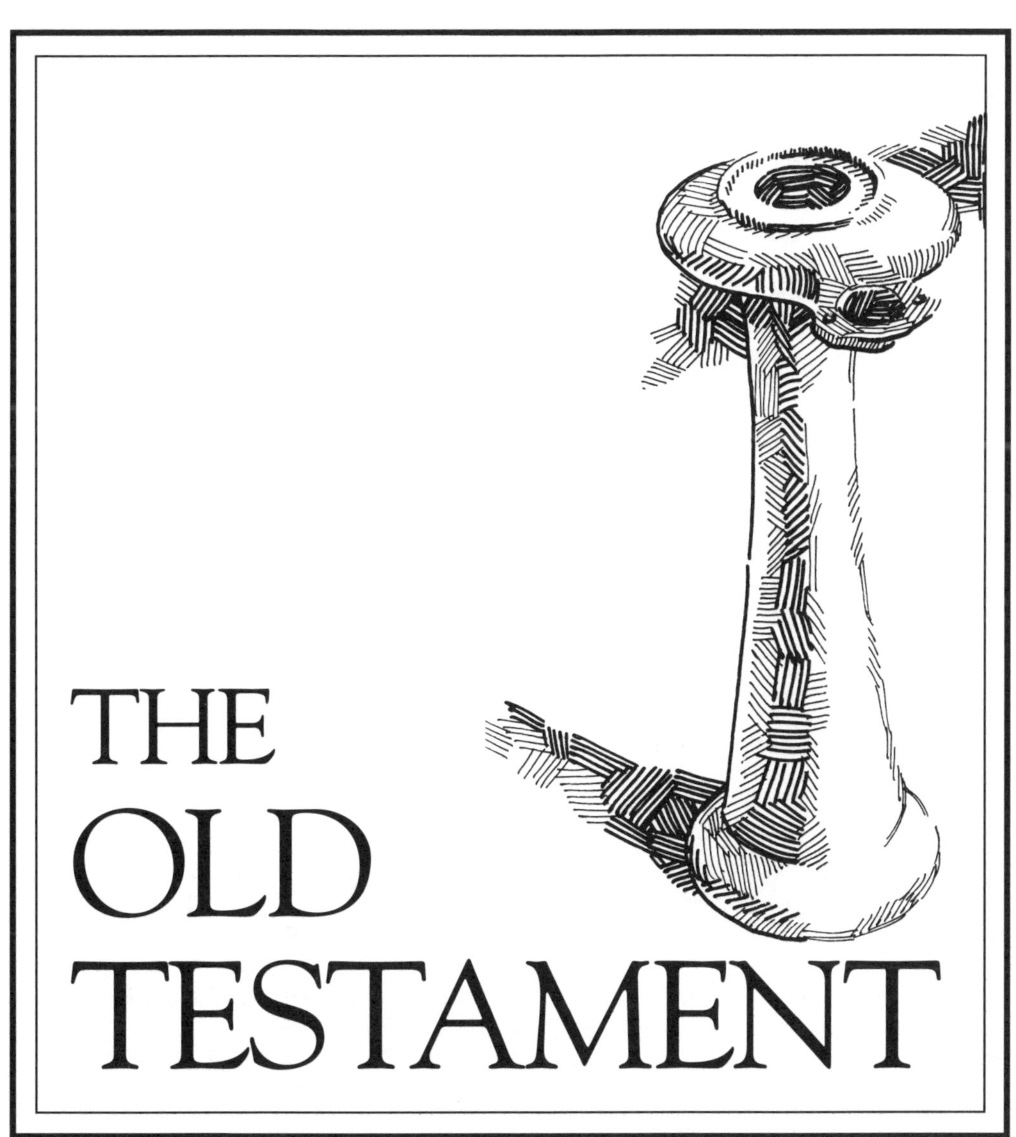

1 The Biblical Word

GATHERING AND PRAYER

(5 minutes)
Begin on time with those who are there. Use the theme word, theme verse, "Our Human Condition," and prayer from the study manual.

VIDEO SEGMENT 1

(20 minutes)
Presenter: Emerson B. Powery

Prepare to View Video
Listen for the reasons we read the Bible and what it means to read the Bible in community.

View Video
Summary of video content:
The reading of Scripture calls us to wrestle with the text in light of the community around us.
Reading the Scriptures in community lets us know we are not alone.
We are part of a host of ancestors who attempted to discern God's activity in the past.
We belong to one another in a global mission seeking to participate in God's mission around the world.
We read the Bible as a means of being faithful.
We read the Bible to hear the stories that help us find our own voices and direction.
The living Word of God helps us discern the spirit of God's Word for our world.

Discuss After Viewing Video
Why do you read the Bible? What can you hope to gain by reading the Bible in community? in the company of your DISCIPLE group?

SCRIPTURE AND STUDY MANUAL

(50 minutes)
Ask persons to recall their first Bible: When and where did you get it? Who gave it to you? What did it mean to you at the time? Then form pairs and tell each other about that first Bible.
Study of Scripture during this session will focus not so much on content as on the type of literature being read. Assign pairs or threes to look at one of the week's passages from the various kinds of biblical literature and try to identify the characteristics of that literature. Join another pair to share ideas. What relationship do you see between the type of literature and the message it carries?

Certain terms in this lesson need to be defined and understood: *canon, Pentateuch,* and *Torah.* Have persons tell a partner their understanding of the terms. Then check your understandings on page 8 of the study manual.
The theme word for this lesson is *authority.* Talk in pairs about the meaning of *authority of Scripture.* In what situations do we pay attention to what Scripture says? Why do we pay attention to Scripture? How does Scripture have authority in my life? What do you expect from the Bible? What does the Bible have a right to expect from its readers?
"If You Want to Know More" suggests memorizing the names of the Old Testament books. Memorize them now as a group. Read a few of the names together at a time; repeat them silently; then, in pairs, recite them several times to each other.

BREAK

(10 minutes)

ENCOUNTER THE WORD

(40 minutes)
Scripture selection: Psalm 84
Ask everyone to read Psalm 84 silently. Then ask them to listen as you read it aloud for sounds, smells, sights, tastes, and touches. With partners, list what you heard or experienced through the senses. (See using all the senses in Bible study, pages 57–61 of *Teaching the Bible to Adults and Youth,* by Dick Murray.)

MARKS OF DISCIPLESHIP

(20 minutes)
Disciples place themselves under the power and authority of Scripture.
Read aloud "Our Human Condition." What is the relationship between the authority of Scripture and the experience described in "Our Human Condition"? Invite volunteers to respond to the questions under "Marks of Discipleship."

CLOSING AND PRAYER

(5 minutes)
Turn to Lesson 2 and check assignments. Write down prayer concerns. Close with prayer.

2 The Creating God

GATHERING AND PRAYER

(5 minutes)

VIDEO SEGMENT 2

(20 minutes)
Presenter: Peter E. Enns

Prepare to View Video

Listen for similarities between the Creation stories of Genesis and the Babylonian creation story.

View Video

Summary of video content:

The Creation stories of Genesis are among many ancient creation stories.

These stories have many similarities: sequence of days, darkness, division of the waters and light existing before the creation of the sun, moon and stars.

But in the Genesis stories, God acts alone and creation is God's doing, not a result of a conflict between many gods.

The Creation stories of Genesis were radical and challenged the ancient world.

Genesis 1 and 2 points out that God is unlike all the other gods and, being made in God's image, humanity is in relationship with God. It is this relationship between God and humanity that will form the backdrop for the rest of the Bible.

Discuss After Viewing Video

What differences do you see between the two Creation accounts in Genesis 1 and Genesis 2? What does understanding Genesis 1–2 as a backdrop for the rest of the Bible say about God and our relationship to God? How does Genesis challenge the Babylonian creation story in its portrayal of God and God's relationship to humans?

SCRIPTURE AND STUDY MANUAL

(50 minutes)

Central to this part of the group meeting are the notes persons have made as they read the assigned Scripture and the study manual. Divide into three groups to talk about what persons have written: Group 1, reading and responses for Days 1 and 2; Group 2, reading and responses for Days 3 and 4; Group 3, reading and responses for Days 5 and 6.

The theme word for the lesson is *wonder*. Ask the same groups to discuss how each of the daily Scripture passages relates to the theme of wonder.

Explore the issue of reclaiming sabbath as a day of rest. Consider these questions: How are we to understand sabbath rest? What changes in attitudes about ourselves and toward God would we need to make if we took seriously the sacredness of sabbath? What changes would we make in our behavior? What benefits would come from treating sabbath as sacred? How would society be affected were Christians to seriously observe sabbath rest?

In considering the two Creation stories, ask for the responses members of the group have made to questions on pages 17–18 in the study manual.

BREAK

(10 minutes)

ENCOUNTER THE WORD

(40 minutes)

Scripture selection: Psalm 8 or Psalm 100

Memorize either of the psalms. Follow these steps: (1) Read the psalm aloud while everyone listens. (2) Read the psalm in unison. (3) With partners repeat the psalm to each other several times. (4) Invite volunteers to recite the psalm from memory. (5) As a total group, recite the psalm from memory. (See memorization, pages 77–80 of *Teaching the Bible to Adults and Youth.*)

MARKS OF DISCIPLESHIP

(20 minutes)

Disciples know they belong to God, that God has claim on them.

The mark of discipleship for this lesson ties to the concern of "Our Human Condition" about whether humans have any importance in a universe so vast. Read "Our Human Condition" aloud. What is the relationship between the experience expressed there and the knowledge and experience of belonging to God? Hear and discuss responses persons have written under "Marks of Discipleship."

CLOSING AND PRAYER

(5 minutes)

Turn to Lesson 3 and write down prayer concerns. Close with a song or prayer.

3 The Rebel People

GATHERING AND PRAYER

(5 minutes)

VIDEO SEGMENT 3

(20 minutes)
Presenter: Peter E. Enns

Prepare to View Video

Listen for the theological messages that Genesis 3–11 communicates and how these chapters describe the problem of sin.

View Video

Summary of video content:

The theological messages of Genesis 3–11 form the basis of the Bible's overall message.

The central question these chapters wrestle with is, "What does God want us to know about God and God's world?"

These early chapters of Genesis connect the story of creation to the story of Israel's ancestors.

The stories describe the fall of humanity and the spread of sin in the world.

These stories of humanity's rebellion and God's response set the stage for the story of God's attempts to reconcile the world.

Discuss After Viewing Video

Through the stories in Genesis 3–11, what does God want us to know about God and God's world? Discuss the similarities and the differences within the stories. The word *sin* is not used in Genesis 3–11; how do those Scriptures describe the problem of sin?

SCRIPTURE AND STUDY MANUAL

(50 minutes)

To provide a perspective from which to talk about the Genesis stories in this lesson, describe these Scriptures as explanations of beginnings, of how things got to be the way they are, of who we are and who God is. Of these stories, ask these questions: What do they teach us about ourselves? about our relationships with others? about our relationship to God?

Read "Our Human Condition" as a starting point for study of the assigned Scriptures and the commentary in the manual. Several theological concepts arise from these Scriptures: the Fall, original sin, the sinful nature of human beings, free will or freedom of choice, confession, and repentance. Form pairs to define the concepts. Then each pair join another to discuss understandings of the concepts. Again in pairs work through the responses called for on pages 22–24.

Provide opportunity for group members to read and discuss their personal "Adam and Eve stories" or work as a group to create a modern-day "Adam and Eve story." After either of these activities, read aloud in unison Psalm 51:1-12 as a confession.

Form two groups of persons to study the effects of sin on persons' lives. Assign one group Jeremiah 8:18–9:11; the second group, 2 Samuel 11:1–12:7. Instruct the groups to read their passage and to identify any evidence of temptation, of rebellion, of alienation, of wickedness, of relationship, of freedom, and of grace. Where any one of these experiences is present, what are its effects on persons' lives?

BREAK

(10 minutes)

ENCOUNTER THE WORD

(40 minutes)

Scripture selection: Genesis 9:1-19

Have one person read Genesis 9:1-19 aloud. In pairs discuss these questions: What does this passage tell us about God? What does this passage tell us about Noah? How are we like Noah? What does this passage tell us about the relationship between God and us? (See theological Bible study, pages 40–44 of *Teaching the Bible to Adults and Youth.*)

MARKS OF DISCIPLESHIP

(20 minutes)

Disciples acknowledge their rebellion, accept responsibility for their sin, and repent.

Assign each of the statements in this section to a trio for response and discussion. Read "Our Human Condition" and the mark of discipleship.

CLOSING AND PRAYER

(5 minutes)

Turn to Lesson 4 and write down prayer concerns. Close with prayer.

4 The Called People

GATHERING AND PRAYER

(5 minutes)

VIDEO SEGMENT 4

(20 minutes)
Presenter: Celia Brewer Sinclair

Prepare to View Video

In covenant, God partners with us to realize God's promises. Listen for ways this partnership is played out in the covenant with Sarah, Abraham, Rebekah and Isaac.

View Video

Summary of video content:

Sarah and Rebekah are often overlooked as partners in fulfilling the covenant promises.

In the story of Sarai and Abram, God makes it clear that they are covenantal partners.

God blesses Abraham and Sarah with a son, Isaac, who is a sign that God's promise will be fulfilled.

The story of Rebekah and Isaac is another case of childlessness followed by a miraculous conception.

Pregnant with twins, Rebekah is visited by God and told of God's plan. She takes the initiative and works to preserve Jacob as the promise, and the future, of Israel.

Discuss After Viewing Video

How do you see God partnering with the characters in these stories to bring about God's promise? What role does each of the characters play?

SCRIPTURE AND STUDY MANUAL

(50 minutes)

You are beginning the study of the history of the people Israel. This lesson introduces the covenant between God and this people with a special mission. This theme will weave its way through the remainder of the study. As you discuss the covenant, pay particular attention to the threefold promise of God's covenant with Abraham.

The history of the chosen people is a history related to geography. Make use of the maps in your Bible and in the study manual.

In pairs talk about the assigned daily readings, looking particularly at God's choice of persons to carry out his purposes and at ways God protected the covenant. Then ask each group member to choose one person from the assigned Scripture who typifies a people called for special mission and tell one other person what is interesting about the chosen person and about how God worked through that person.

In groups of three or four discuss the questions calling for response in "The Bible Teaching."

Hear reports on covenant if persons did additional research suggested in the study manual.

BREAK

(10 minutes)

ENCOUNTER THE WORD

(40 minutes)

Scripture selection: Genesis 32:9-32

Hear the passage read aloud. Then form teams of three for study. Divide the passage among the three for individual work using these questions: What does this passage say about God? What does this passage say about human beings? What does this passage say about the relationship between God and human beings? Then work through the entire passage together. (See theological Bible study, pages 40–44 of *Teaching the Bible to Adults and Youth.*)

MARKS OF DISCIPLESHIP

(20 minutes)

Disciples respond to God's call to enter the covenant community of faith and express commitment to the covenant through the tithe.

Read aloud the statement of "Our Human Condition." Then discuss this question: What kind of call has the power to draw persons beyond themselves?

Discuss together the responses persons have made to the questions in "Marks of Discipleship." Raise the question of whether or not group members are willing to covenant together to tithe for the remainder of their study of DISCIPLE. Perhaps that is one call that would take persons beyond themselves.

CLOSING AND PRAYER

(5 minutes)

Turn to Lesson 5 and write down prayer concerns. Close with prayer.

5 God Hears the Cry

GATHERING AND PRAYER

(5 minutes)

VIDEO SEGMENT 5

(20 minutes)
Presenter: Thomas B. Dozeman

Prepare to View Video

Listen for the importance of memory both for God and for humanity and how memory is crucial to the story and the celebration of Passover.

View Video

Summary of video content:

In the Book of Exodus, those now living as slaves in Egypt have no memory of God or God's salvation history.

God enters human history to save the Israelite people from slavery and death, and to create a new future by fulfilling past promises to their ancestors.

Through Moses, God leads the Israelites out of the land of Egypt and through the Red Sea.

Why is the night of Passover different from all other nights? The Passover creates hope since the recounting of the past salvation of God also leads to a future vision, when all evil will be destroyed like Pharaoh and his army.

Discuss After Viewing Video

How is Exodus a story of divine memory and action? Why is the night of Passover different from all other nights? Why does it have significance for Christians as well as Jews?

SCRIPTURE AND STUDY MANUAL

(50 minutes)

The importance of the Exodus event cannot be overemphasized. Israel's history is always viewed through the lens of the Exodus. Raise the question of what that fact says about Israel's understanding of their relationship to God.

To get a sense of the people who played a leading role in the Exodus, name the characters one at a time and ask persons to list all the words they can think of to describe that person. The characters are Shiphrah and Puah, Jochebed, Miriam, Pharaoh's daughter, Moses, Aaron, Pharaoh.

Together, identify and list turning points in the story of the Exodus, beginning with the rise of the new king and ending with the entry into the Sinai wilderness. At each point discuss this question: As Israel looked back on the Exodus, how did they understand God to be at work at this point?

Another way to deal with the same information would be to tell the story around the circle. The first person would start the story and take it as far as he or she wants to go. The next person would pick up the story and do likewise. The storytelling would continue around the circle as many times as necessary to complete the story.

BREAK

(10 minutes)

ENCOUNTER THE WORD

(40 minutes)

Scripture selection: Exodus 3:1–4:17

Ask everyone to read the passage silently, write down new insights and questions, and then talk with others about what they found. In pairs or threes study the passage using these questions: What happens in the story? What do you think the writer wanted to convey in this account? What seems to be the central idea? What meaning does this passage have for the church today? Individually, respond to this question: What is the meaning of the passage for me? (See depth Bible study, pages 35–39 of *Teaching the Bible to Adults and Youth.*)

MARKS OF DISCIPLESHIP

(20 minutes)

Disciples hear and obey God's call to be bearers of God's message of deliverance.

Ask half the group to read "Our Human Condition" aloud, and the other half to respond with the mark of discipleship. Then work through the questions under "Marks of Discipleship." Consider what God's message of deliverance is that the faithful disciple must bear today.

CLOSING AND PRAYER

(5 minutes)

Turn to Lesson 6 and write down prayer concerns. Close with prayer.

6 God Sends the Law

GATHERING AND PRAYER

(5 minutes)

VIDEO SEGMENT 6

(20 minutes)
Presenter: Cheryl B. Anderson

Prepare to View Video

Listen for the purpose of the Law and the difference between the letter of the Law and the spirit of the Law.

View Video

Summary of video content:

God sends the Law for the journey from slavery in Egypt to freedom in the Promised Land. The Law is set within the context of the Torah. The narratives tell us why we should follow the laws.

The Decalogue or the Ten Commandments offer general principles concerning what is required to live in relationship with God. It is possible to know the letter of the Law but fail to understand the spirit of the Law.

The rationale for the Law brings responsibilities under God's covenant and the requirement to act in certain ways before God and with families and neighbors alike.

To be a person of faith is not just a matter of what we believe, it is also a matter of how we behave.

Discuss After Viewing Video

How can understanding the spirit of the Law affect the way we interpret and live out the Law, especially the Ten Commandments?

SCRIPTURE AND STUDY MANUAL

(50 minutes)

Guide the discussion of the assigned Scripture and the observations and questions persons have toward three goals: to understand the meaning and function of Torah, to discover the sense in which Torah defined the Israelites as a distinct people, and to learn the nature of God made evident in the Law God gave to the people. Write the goals on newsprint and display them as persons work.

In pairs review the assigned daily Scriptures and notes made about the Scriptures in order to discuss these questions: What was the purpose of the Law? How did the requirements of the Law make the Israelites a distinct people? What did the laws God gave the people teach the people about God? Follow this discussion with discussion of responses called for in "The Bible Teaching."

These Scriptures on the Law also provide us a close look at Moses the lawgiver. Assign passages to small groups to see what they can discover about Moses as the receiver of the Law from God and the bringer of the Law to the people.

Several passages in the assigned Scripture are worthy of memorizing. Two are the Ten Commandments, which some already may have memorized, and Deuteronomy 6:4-9, which is an elaboration of the first commandment.

BREAK

(10 minutes)

ENCOUNTER THE WORD

(40 minutes)

Scripture selection: Deuteronomy 8

Read Deuteronomy 8 aloud as others follow along in their Bibles. Work in groups of three to discuss these questions: What does this passage tell us about God? What does this passage tell us about people? What does this passage tell us about the relationship between God and people? (See theological Bible study, pages 40–44 of *Teaching the Bible to Adults and Youth*.)

MARKS OF DISCIPLESHIP

(20 minutes)

Disciples keep God's law by doing it.

The responses called for in this section relate directly to human needs described in "Our Human Condition." Discuss responses. Invite several persons to read their descriptions of who the disciple is according to the Scripture for this lesson.

CLOSING AND PRAYER

(5 minutes)

Turn to Lesson 7 and write down prayer concerns. Close with prayer.

7 When God Draws Near

GATHERING AND PRAYER

(5 minutes)

VIDEO SEGMENT 7

(20 minutes)
Presenter: Cheryl B. Anderson

Prepare to View Video

The covenantal relationship between God and God's people is comprised of both the Law and the liturgy. Listen for what Anderson means by that.

View Video

Summary of video content:

The covenantal relationship with God and God's people called for special responsibilities: to build a structure that would allow God to dwell among them and to observe a liturgy that would help them live up to their responsibilities.

The sacrificial system provided a type of communication between the people and God. Through the act of atonement, the process of achieving and maintaining oneness and reconciliation with God, a right relationship with God was achieved.

The covenantal relationship with God reminds us of our ongoing responsibility to God.

These priestly laws also remind us of the importance of worship and that the way we live our lives should itself be an act of worship.

Discuss After Viewing Video

What did receiving the Law and the liturgy at the same time accomplish for the Israelites? What is the connection between atonement and the Law? between atonement and the liturgy?

SCRIPTURE AND STUDY MANUAL

(50 minutes)

Introduce and explore Hebrew worship in relation to three topics: need for worship, place of worship, elements in worship.

Need for worship: Introduce the subjects of guilt and sin by reading aloud "Our Human Condition." Also look at the need of persons to give thanks to God and the recognition of worship as interwoven with all of life, not something added on to life.

Place of worship: Look at the drawing and the design of the Tabernacle on pages 54 and 222 in the study manual. Identify the different parts. Exodus 25–27 describes the Tabernacle and its furnishings.

Elements in worship: Opportunity to remember, to ask forgiveness, and to give thanks are described in the study manual as *remembrance, atonement, thanksgiving*. Discuss the questions related to those ideas in the study manual. These words provide opportunity for definition, for theological interpretation of atonement, and for discussion of the parallels in Hebrew and Christian worship in relation to Passover and the death of Jesus as symbols of deliverance and salvation.

In pairs, discuss this question: What means and opportunities do Christians have in worship for affirming and reaffirming their faith?

BREAK

(10 minutes)

ENCOUNTER THE WORD

(40 minutes)

Scripture selection: Exodus 40:16-38

Ask everyone to read Exodus 40:16-38 silently. Then read the passage aloud while group members listen for sounds, smells, sights, tastes, and touches. With partners, list instances involving the senses and discuss this question: What can we learn about God from this Scripture? (See using all the senses in Bible study, pages 57–61 of *Teaching the Bible to Adults and Youth.*)

MARKS OF DISCIPLESHIP

(20 minutes)

Disciples commit themselves to corporate worship.

Use questions in this section of the study manual to help persons discuss their attitudes toward and commitment to corporate worship. Invite persons to talk about whether their sense of need is similar to that described in thc study manual.

CLOSING AND PRAYER

(5 minutes)

Turn to Lesson 8 and write down prayer concerns. Close with prayer.

8 The People Without a King

GATHERING AND PRAYER

(5 minutes)

VIDEO SEGMENT 8

(20 minutes)
Presenter: Kathleen A. Farmer

Prepare to View Video

Listen for why God's chosen people lost the land God promised them. What role did Joshua and the judges play in Israel's experience?

View Video

Summary of video content:

The Promised Land was lost because God's chosen people and their ancestors failed to keep the covenant they had made with God.

The narrative of Israel's experience in the land of Canaan is called the Deuteronomistic History. This narration reads more like a confession of sin than a celebration of Israel's past.

Joshua's warnings of keeping the covenant resulted in a renewal of the covenant. However, the period of history from the death of Joshua to the beginning of David's reign was an endless cycle, moving from sin to punishment and back again.

Israel's failure to acknowledge the rule of God allowed evil to reign supreme.

Discuss After Viewing Video

"In those days, there was no king in Israel; people did what was right in their own eyes." How does this statement describe how God's chosen people came to lose their promised land? What role did Joshua and the judges play in Israel's experience?

SCRIPTURE AND STUDY MANUAL

(50 minutes)

In establishing the background for study of the conquest and settlement of the land, include a review of Joshua's own history under the leadership of Moses and then as Moses' successor. Go all the way back to the Exodus.

Divide the group into four small groups to study Joshua and Judges. Make the following assignments: Group 1: Days 1 and 2, focusing on the fall of Jericho; Group 2: Day 3, Deborah and Barak; Group 3: Day 4, Gideon; Group 4: Day 5, Samson. Instruct the groups to discuss their assigned Scripture and their daily notes in relation to these questions: How was this event viewed from the perspective of Israel's faith? What was the condition of the covenant between God and the people at this point? How would the people themselves have described who God was and how they related to God?

Identify and talk about individual judges. Use these questions: What kind of person does God choose to carry out God's purposes? Why do you think God chose this person for leadership?

Running throughout Joshua and Judges is an alternating pattern of obedience and disobedience. Identify some accounts that fit this pattern.

BREAK

(10 minutes)

ENCOUNTER THE WORD

(40 minutes)

Scripture selection: Joshua 24:1-28

Ask someone to read Joshua 24:1-28 aloud as others follow in their Bibles. Then discuss these questions: What does this passage tell us about God? What does this passage tell us about human beings? What does this passage tell us about the relationship between God and human beings? (See theological Bible study, pages 40–44 of *Teaching the Bible to Adults and Youth.*)

MARKS OF DISCIPLESHIP

(20 minutes)

Disciples provide a sense of direction and purpose through godly, obedient leadership.

In considering "Our Human Condition" in relation to the "Marks of Discipleship," discuss this question: How do the political disorder and confusion and the obedience and disobedience in our day compare with that of the time of the judges? Discuss the questions under "Marks of Discipleship" using the written responses of group members.

CLOSING AND PRAYER

(5 minutes)

Turn to Lesson 9 and write down prayer concerns. Close with prayer.

9 The People With a King

GATHERING AND PRAYER

(5 minutes)

VIDEO SEGMENT 9

(20 minutes)
Presenter: Kathleen A. Farmer

Prepare to View Video

Listen for how the biblical historian, writing from the perspective of the Exile, told the story of the Israelites' experience with their kings.

View Video

Summary of video content:

Threatened by invasion from their enemies, God's people saw military victory as their only hope.

They asked Samuel to appoint a king to govern them like other nations were governed.

Reluctantly, a king was chosen. In succession, Saul, David, and Solomon served as king.

The unification of the tribes was short-lived and the monarchy was divided between the Northern Kingdom of Israel and the Southern Kingdom of Judah. The classical prophets were active during this period of the Divided Monarchy.

Political instability eventually led to the fall of both Israel and Judah.

Exiled in Babylon, historians realized that each of the kings of Israel and Judah contributed in some way to their nation's downhill slide toward destruction.

Discuss After Viewing Video

Why did the people desire a king? What was their experience of a king? What impact did writing from the perspective of the Exile have on how the history of the kings and God's people was told?

SCRIPTURE AND STUDY MANUAL

(50 minutes)

Review the events that led up to the people's demand for a king. (See the chart of biblical history on page 63.) Talk about what this demand would eventually do to the understanding that God was the ruler of the Israelite nation.

Look at the four characters in this lesson one at a time. Make use of related Scripture passages and information from the study manual. In each case there is a tension between the person's desire to serve God and the effects of position and power. Try to identify that tension. After discussing each person, make a list of the person's strengths and weaknesses.

Discuss these questions: In what ways can you identify with the desires and weaknesses of these biblical people? How do we modern people who are trying to be faithful to the one God experience the lure of other gods?

Hear reports from members who did research on Solomon's Temple.

BREAK

(10 minutes)

ENCOUNTER THE WORD

(40 minutes)

Scripture selection: 1 Kings 9:1-9

Read aloud 1 Kings 9:1-9 while others follow along in their Bibles. Ask everyone to write down the insights they received from the Scripture. For each of the next three steps, work individually and then with a partner. Find a different partner for each step. (1) Write down the central idea of the passage. (2) Write down the meaning the passage has for today's world. (3) Write down the personal message of the passage. (See depth Bible study, pages 35–39 of *Teaching the Bible to Adults and Youth.*)

MARKS OF DISCIPLESHIP

(20 minutes)

Disciples maintain a perspective on leadership that supports and respects godly leaders but give true allegiance only to God.

The first three questions in this section have a direct connection to the statement of "Our Human Condition." In answering the questions, look for clues in the condition.

CLOSING AND PRAYER

(5 minutes)

Turn to Lesson 10 and write down prayer concerns. Close with prayer.

10 God Warns the People

GATHERING AND PRAYER

(5 minutes)

VIDEO SEGMENT 10

(20 minutes)
Presenter: Jin Hee Han

Prepare to View Video

Listen for the condition and response of the world when the prophetic voice of Elijah is raised, calling for faithfulness and justice.

View Video

Summary of video content:

The historian of First and Second Kings never measures a royal reign by how powerful the king may have been in the world, but by how faithful he was to the Lord.

Given this criteria, none of the kings in the north, and few in the south, get a passing grade. According to the historian, they did what was evil in the sight of the Lord. Ahab, in particular, was denounced for introducing idol worship.

At this low point in Israel's history, Elijah hoped to turn the heart of the people back to the one and only true God.

On Mount Carmel, Elijah asked the people to make a choice about who they would worship: God or Baal. When Baal is silent and God answers with a consuming fire, Elijah's message is heard.

Discuss After Viewing Video

What must be happening in the world in order for a prophetic voice to be raised? What must happen for people to respond to that prophetic voice?

SCRIPTURE AND STUDY MANUAL

(50 minutes)

Two kinds of information are important as background for studying this lesson: (1) an understanding of who the prophets were, how they related to God, and what their message was; (2) the time periods of the prophets and of the events treated in the lesson. Review "The Bible Teaching" section and see the chart on page 85.

Guide groups of three through the assigned Scripture using these questions: Who is the prophet described in this passage? What is the nature of the disobedience to which the prophet is speaking? What warning does the prophet give? How do the people respond? Encourage persons to bring into the discussions information and questions from their daily reading and study.

Unwillingness to hear the word of warning is not unique to Elijah's time. As the group answers the questions on page 76 of the study manual, have them identify and discuss the parallels between that time and our time.

BREAK

(10 minutes)

ENCOUNTER THE WORD

(40 minutes)

Scripture selection: 1 Kings 19:1-18

Try mental drama. Read 1 Kings 19:1-18 aloud. Clarify the setting, the characters, and what's going on in the story. Ask persons to close their eyes. Then guide their thinking and imagining with questions about what Elijah thought, how he felt, what he thought about God. Give time for thought after each question. No responses are made aloud. Talk in pairs or threes about the experience. What new insights did persons have into Elijah and into the story? (See mental drama, pages 102–04 of *Teaching the Bible to Adults and Youth.*)

MARKS OF DISCIPLESHIP

(20 minutes)

Disciples recognize and listen to prophetic voices raised about community, nation, and world and at times become the prophetic voice.

Read the statement of "Our Human Condition" and talk about whether it accurately reflects persons' experience. Then discuss this question: Why do we prefer not to listen to most warnings?

Because most persons do not think of themselves as prophets, group members may hesitate to respond openly to the last item in this section. Encourage persons to volunteer what they have written.

CLOSING AND PRAYER

(5 minutes)

Turn to Lesson 11 and write down prayer concerns. Close with prayer.

11 God Punishes the People

GATHERING AND PRAYER

(5 minutes)

VIDEO SEGMENT 11

(20 minutes)
Presenter: Jin Hee Han

Prepare to View Video

Listen for the messages of hope and warning.

View Video

Summary of video content:

Judah experienced religious reform during the reign of Josiah:

- Restoration and rededication of the Temple
- Discovery of the book of the Law led to a renewal and reinstitution of religious rites
- Purging of alien cultic objects from Temple and demolition of local sanctuaries and high places
- Institution of a national celebration of Passover

After the death of Josiah, the nation went downhill quickly, and Jeremiah warned of God's judgment.

Jerusalem was destroyed and the people were taken into exile. Yet, even in the face of the catastrophe and despair, Jeremiah preached and practiced hope.

Discuss After Viewing Video

"Both blessings and disasters are in the hands of the Lord." How do you respond to that statement? According to Second Kings, which gets the people's attention: blessings or disasters? Why? What is Jeremiah's response?

SCRIPTURE AND STUDY MANUAL

(50 minutes)

To get the situation in the Scripture before the group, work together to compile a list of the key events or situations in 2 Kings 17–25. The emphasis here should be on getting a picture of the actions and attitudes of the people that were leading to their downfall and exile. The time charts on pages 84 and 85 will remind group members of events and their sequence, and the maps in their Bibles will aid in locating events related to the Northern and Southern Kingdoms.

Against that background, try to sense the distress of the prophets in having to deliver God's warning of the coming judgment. At the same time, they had a message of hope to give to the people. Invite the group members to put themselves first in the place of the prophets and then in the place of the people who heard the words of the prophets. Identify in the assigned Scriptures five or six passages that are warnings and five or six passages that are words of hope. Alternate the reading aloud of the two kinds of passages. Group 1 will read a warning, to which Group 2 will respond by reading a passage of hope. At the end of the reading, ask persons to talk about the feelings they had as they read and listened to the words of warning and the words of hope.

Hear reports if persons did research on the Jews in exile.

BREAK

(10 minutes)

ENCOUNTER THE WORD

(40 minutes)

Scripture selection: Jeremiah 24

In groups of three or four read Jeremiah 24 silently. Then study the passage using these questions: What do you think the writer intended to say for God to those to whom it was written? What does this text have to say to the church in our day? If I took this passage seriously, what change would I have to make in my life? (See depth Bible study, 35–39 of *Teaching the Bible to Adults and Youth.*)

MARKS OF DISCIPLESHIP

(20 minutes)

Disciples accept consequences of their sin, seek forgiveness, look for healing and new opportunities for faithfulness.

Read the statement of "Our Human Condition" aloud. Ask the group members to identify any parts of the statement that are untrue in their experience and to adapt the statement to make it true for them. Then in pairs respond to the first two blocks of information in this section of the study manual. Discuss the last two questions in the total group.

CLOSING AND PRAYER

(5 minutes)

Turn to Lesson 12 and write down prayer concerns. Close with prayer.

12 God Restores the People

GATHERING AND PRAYER

(5 minutes)

VIDEO SEGMENT 12

(20 minutes)
Presenter: Julia M. O'Brien

Prepare to View Video

Listen for views on God's punishment and the role of the "suffering servant."

View Video

Summary of video content:

God holds the people of Judah accountable for their sins. God used the Babylonians to punish them.

Second Isaiah (the writer of Isaiah 40–55) brings a word of hope. The God who acted to destroy Judah was about to restore it.

The restoration would be at the hands of Cyrus, king of the Persians, and through the life of an unknown figure called the "suffering servant," who suffers innocently and whose suffering benefits others.

Suffering is not necessarily the sign of God's disfavor and punishment; rather, God may well redeem suffering for the sake of the world. God can work a redemptive purpose in even the most broken of persons and situations.

Jeremiah 31 affirms that after the exile God will establish a new covenant with the people, a covenant written on people's hearts.

Discuss After Viewing Video

The same God who holds people accountable for their behaviors is also gracious and forgiving. How was this played out in the life of the people of Judah? How is this still played out in the life of God's people?

SCRIPTURE AND STUDY MANUAL

(50 minutes)

The theme word for this lesson is *comfort*. Hear reports from persons who did research on the meaning of the word *comfort*. Then, in pairs, scan "The Bible Teaching" section for ways comfort is expressed and offered. Hear each pair tell what they discovered.

Throughout the assigned Scripture are powerful word pictures that point to the restoration of Israel. Have teams of three go through the Scriptures for each day and locate some of these word pictures. Read the word pictures aloud in the total group to gain a feeling of the comfort that was in them for Israel.

BREAK

(10 minutes)

ENCOUNTER THE WORD

(40 minutes)

Scripture selection: Isaiah 45:1-13

Read aloud Isaiah 45:1-13. Then in threes discuss these questions: What does this passage tell us about God? What does this passage tell us about human beings represented by Cyrus? What does this passage tell us about the relationship between God and Cyrus as a human being? (See theological Bible study, pages 40–44 of *Teaching the Bible to Adults and Youth*.)

MARKS OF DISCIPLESHIP

(20 minutes)

Disciples choose to serve rather than to despair when suffering the consequences of sin.

Ask members of the group to read the statement of "Our Human Condition" silently. Invite any who are willing to do so to recall in a sentence or two a time when they faced the choice between service and despair and to say which choice they made. Give opportunity for volunteers to share their responses under "Marks of Discipleship."

Notice that in the story of Ezekiel and the wheels, Ezekiel's understanding of God was enlarged. In teams recall other accounts in Scripture where persons' understanding of God grew. Share personal experiences of growth in understanding of God.

CLOSING AND PRAYER

(5 minutes)

Turn to Lesson 13 and write down prayer concerns. Call attention to the sequence for reading and writing. Close with prayer.

13 Songs of the Heart

GATHERING AND PRAYER

(5 minutes)

VIDEO SEGMENT 13

(20 minutes)
Presenter: Melody D. Knowles

Prepare to View Video

Assign two listening teams. One team listens for the characteristics and function of the psalms of praise. The other team listens for the characteristics and function of the psalms of lament.

View Video

Summary of video content:

The Psalms mirror our hearts and speak our deepest thoughts. They can teach our hearts about who God is and what God has done. They also teach us how to pray.

Psalms of praise (Psalm 147 and 116)

- Often used in corporate worship
- Two types: descriptive—praise the attributes of God; declarative—give thanks for a specific act
- Teach us who God is

Psalms of lament (Psalm 13 and 74)

- Two types: solitary voice—"rescue me"; corporate voice—God is asked to intervene
- Prayers to God asking for help

Discuss After Viewing Video

Ask the listening teams to report what they heard. Why do we so often turn to the psalms? How have the psalms taught you to pray?

SCRIPTURE AND STUDY MANUAL

(50 minutes)

To make the point that we are known completely by God, read aloud in unison Psalm 139.

In working through the assigned Scripture and daily notes, encourage persons to talk about the feelings they had as they read the Psalms and their insights about who God is and who they are in relation to God.

Form teams of three to talk about their written responses to the questions in the study manual.

Part of the joy in reading and studying the Psalms is that they put us in touch with ourselves and with our humanity. Suggest that each person in the group choose a psalm that speaks for her or him and read it aloud to the group.

Two other ways of enjoying the Psalms would be to memorize a psalm in the group or to sing some hymns based on psalms. Together select a psalm or portion of a psalm to memorize. Before memorizing it, talk about what it says, what it means, and how it mirrors human emotions. See pages 77–80 of *Teaching the Bible to Adults and Youth* for procedures on memorizing Scripture. Hymns based on psalms are suggested in the study manual. With each hymn you sing, read the related psalm.

BREAK

(10 minutes)

ENCOUNTER THE WORD

(40 minutes)

Scripture selection: Psalm 22

In teams of three, work through the psalm in blocks of verses using these questions: What does the psalm tell us about God? What does the psalm tell us about us? What does the psalm tell us about the relationship between God and us? (See theological Bible study, pages 40–44 of *Teaching the Bible to Adults and Youth.*)

MARKS OF DISCIPLESHIP

(20 minutes)

Disciples trust God with all their thoughts and feelings.

Notice that "Our Human Condition" says what we know about ourselves. The theme verse says what God knows about us. How do we then achieve the mark of discipleship for this lesson? Why are we often uncomfortable and hesitant about expressing our anger or negative feelings to God?

CLOSING AND PRAYER

(5 minutes)

Turn to Lesson 14 and write down prayer concerns. Alert persons to the writing called for in Lesson 14. Close with prayer.

14 The Righteous Are Like a Tree

GATHERING AND PRAYER

(5 minutes)

VIDEO SEGMENT 14

(20 minutes)
Presenter: Melody D. Knowles

Prepare to View Video

Listen for the major concerns of the postexilic community.

View Video

Summary of video content:

The victory of Cyrus brought not only a new political order to the ancient Near East, but it also brought new theological choices for God's people.

Major concerns:

- Temple worship. Some return to build. Some stay behind to help fund the project.
- Defining community boundaries in the midst of various groups: returning exiles, exiles living outside the land (Diaspora), adversaries, and foreigners.
- How to live faithfully and practice righteousness

Deeply influenced by international traditions, the Book of Proverbs suggests that right living comes not by excluding the foreigner, but by adapting some of the insights of other traditions, and marshalling them under "the fear of the Lord."

Discuss After Viewing Video

What were the major concerns of the postexilic community and how did the people deal with them?

SCRIPTURE AND STUDY MANUAL

(50 minutes)

The theme word for the lesson is *right living*. Begin by asking the group to define right living and to say why it is called for. Discuss this question: What is different about understanding right living as its own reward and understanding right living *for* reward?

Notes on Scripture assignments for Days 2–4 will relate to the written work on biblical guidelines for walking a godly path. Ask each person in turn to respond to one item. Where Scripture references are involved, ask persons to read the Scripture and the guideline arising from it.

Identify Proverbs as Wisdom Literature and work together to list the characteristics of Wisdom Literature. Probably several persons in the group underlined portions of Proverbs as they read. To get a feel for the ideas persons thought particularly important, ask for volunteers to read some of the verses they underlined.

To provide a context for talking about why the Jews wanted to obey perfectly and to live rightly, recall the history of Israel from the time of Abraham and up to the period of Ezra and Nehemiah. Use the chart on biblical history on page 105. Then read aloud in unison or have someone read aloud Nehemiah 8:1–9:5; 10:28-39. Discuss the questions, reflections, and insights persons recorded as they read these passages during their weekly study.

You may want to use the suggestions under "If You Want to Know More" in the study manual.

BREAK

(10 minutes)

ENCOUNTER THE WORD

(40 minutes)

Scripture selection: Psalm 112

Read Psalm 112 in unison. Work in pairs to identify major ideas in the passage. Then have persons work individually to put the passage into their own words. (See paraphrasing, pages 71–76 of *Teaching the Bible to Adults and Youth.*)

MARKS OF DISCIPLESHIP

(20 minutes)

Disciples strive to live in harmony with God's laws even though obedience is costly.

Begin this section by reading the statement of "Our Human Condition." Then ask these questions: How accurate is this statement in your experience? What are the costs of right living today? Discuss the questions under "Marks of Discipleship" calling for written responses.

CLOSING AND PRAYER

(5 minutes)

Turn to Lesson 15 and write down prayer concerns. Look together at the assignment for the coming week. Close with prayer.

15 When Trouble Comes

Note to the teacher: Much of the group meeting will be spent reading aloud an excerpt from Job. "Scripture and Study Manual" includes the time usually given to "Encounter the Word." Decide ahead of time whom you want to read the parts and call those persons to get their agreement.

Decide whether you want the readers to sit in front of the group as they read or to read from where they are seated. Some persons may want to follow the reading in their manual and mark ideas as they listen; others may want simply to listen.

GATHERING AND PRAYER

(5 minutes)

VIDEO SEGMENT 15

(20 minutes)
Presenter: Mark Price

Prepare to View Video

Listen for the following responses to Job's suffering: Job's, Job's friends, and God's.

View Video

Summary of video content:

A study of the Book of Job presents a number of challenges:

- Reconciling the compliant Job of the prologue with the complaining Job of the epilogue
- Understanding the complex depiction of God
- Making sense of the sophisticated and often ambiguous poetic language

The book begins and ends with a prose narrative. A long poem stands in between, written as a conversation between Job and three friends. A monologue by Elihu follows. God then speaks to Job out of the whirlwind, and the poetry ends with a last word from Job.

The opening question, "Does Job fear God for nothing?" is not the only question on the table. Job wants to know why God should be feared at all if God is indeed so oblivious to injustice and suffering.

His friends insist that Job must have sinned and is getting what he deserves.

Job demands an answer from God. God answers with a litany of questions and imperatives. In response, Job sees himself and God in a new way.

Discuss After Viewing Video

What do the responses of Job, Job's friends and God convey about the message of the book? How do you respond to Job's suffering?

SCRIPTURE AND STUDY MANUAL

(90 minutes)

Before the reading of the excerpt from Job, remind group members of what their task will be after hearing the reading. Put these three steps on newsprint and call attention to them:

1. to try to identify the different kinds of counsel offered by Job's friends;
2. to observe how their explanations are still used today;
3. to consider the sense in which the explanations are partly true but not completely appropriate.

Read the Job Excerpt

After hearing the reading of Job, work first in teams of three to try to identify the various arguments in the counsel given by Job's friends. Write them on page 112 of the manual. Notes made during daily study would be useful at this point. After the teams have worked for a set period of time, talk in the total group about issues in Steps 2 and 3 above.

BREAK

(10 minutes)

MARKS OF DISCIPLESHIP

(20 minutes)

Disciples trust God in the face of unexplained suffering.

Read the statement of "Our Human Condition" and ask these questions: What is to keep us from becoming bitter when we do not understand what is happening to us and why? How can we learn to trust God when we have no answers? Hear responses persons have written in "Marks of Discipleship" in the study manual.

CLOSING AND PRAYER

(5 minutes)

Turn to Lesson 16 and write down prayer concerns. Close with prayer.

16 People Hope for a Savior

GATHERING AND PRAYER

(5 minutes)

VIDEO SEGMENT 16

(20 minutes)
Presenter: Daniel L. Smith-Christopher

Prepare to View Video

Divide into two listening teams. Ask one team to listen for information related to the hero stories in Daniel 1–6 and the other team for information related to the visions in Daniel 7–12.

View Video

Summary of video content:
Daniel is composed of two kinds of literature:
- The hero stories (1–6)
  - Arose in circumstances characterized by Diaspora existence, cross-cultural contact, and uneven distribution of power
  - Contain a call to resist and defy foreign power (i.e. refusing the king's food and wine)
  - Message—Remain faithful in times of trial
- The visions (7–12)
  - Describe conflict
  - Involve both earthly and heavenly figures
  - Give reassurance that God is in charge
  - Message—Be boldly defiant because God has ultimate dominion over all.

The Book of Daniel calls us to speak truth to power.

Discuss After Viewing Video

Ask the listening teams to report what they heard. Discuss the overall theme of Daniel.

SCRIPTURE AND STUDY MANUAL

(50 minutes)

Review the commentary in the study manual to get a picture of the time in which Daniel was written, the period of Antiochus Epiphanes IV. Then together recall what the period of the Babylonian Exile was like. Discuss this question: Why do you think the writer of Daniel thought the period of the Exile a good setting for his message?

For the themes and characteristics of apocalyptic literature listed in the study manual to have meaning for group members, guide them in reading Daniel 7. Read the passage aloud. Identify the apocalyptic themes and characteristics used there.

In order to understand the message of hope in Daniel, first try to sense what the Jews were feeling and experiencing during the persecutions of Antiochus Epiphanes. Then ask groups of three or four persons to identify possible violations of Christian practice and faith that would be comparable to the violations of Jewish practice and faith. Identify and imagine the feelings Christians might have in such a situation. Then ask this question: What message of hope would Christians hear in Daniel?

Look for hope in Daniel. Assign one day's Scripture from Daniel to each of four teams. Instruct each team to describe for the group one picture of hope they find in that Scripture.

BREAK

(10 minutes)

ENCOUNTER THE WORD

(40 minutes)

Scripture selection: Isaiah 65:17-25

Read Isaiah 65:17-25 as a responsive reading. Then ask the group to listen for sounds, sights, smells, touches, and tastes as you read the passage aloud. With partners, talk about which senses the Scripture appealed to and describe to each other feelings while hearing the Scripture. (See using all the senses in Bible study, pages 57–61 of *Teaching the Bible to Adults and Youth.*)

MARKS OF DISCIPLESHIP

(20 minutes)

Disciples sense their unity with the historic people of God and live in hope with a vision of God's kingdom.

Read aloud "Our Human Condition." Then discuss responses to the questions in "Marks of Discipleship." In responding to the last item in this section, talk about its relationship to the statement of "Our Human Condition."

CLOSING AND PRAYER

(5 minutes)

Turn to Lesson 17 and write down prayer concerns. Look at daily assignments. Locate articles on history in your Bible. Close with prayer.

17 The Time of Transition

GATHERING AND PRAYER

(5 minutes)

VIDEO SEGMENT 17

(20 minutes)
Presenter: Sidnie W. Crawford

Prepare to View Video

Listen for the challenges facing the Jews during the Persian period and the messages of the stories of Esther and Jonah.

View Video

Summary of video content:

The Persian period was a time of transition for the Jews. During this time, more Jews lived outside the historical land of Israel than inside it. These circumstances created challenges for the Jews. The stories of Esther and Jonah sought to address the questions Jews were facing.

The purpose of the story of Esther was to teach a lesson: how Jews were to function successfully in a Gentile world. Without mentioning God or religion, the writer promotes the idea that Jews and Gentiles can live together harmoniously and with mutual respect in the Diaspora world.

The story of Jonah tells a deceptively simple story about a prophet named Jonah. Through use of broad humor, the author makes a serious point and addresses the question, "Is God the God only of the Israelites, or does God's power extend to other people?" The answer is God is the God of both Jews and Gentiles, and God's power and mercy extends over the whole world.

Discuss After Viewing Video

During the Persian period, the Jews experienced a time of transition and multiple challenges. How did the messages of Esther and Jonah address these challenges?

SCRIPTURE AND STUDY MANUAL

(50 minutes)

The theme word for this lesson is different in kind from other theme words in the study. Talk about what it means and how it fits.

To get acquainted with the books of Esther and Jonah, the period in which they were written, and their purpose, look together at their introductory pages in the Bible. Distinguish between the writer of the Book of Jonah and the figure Jonah in the story.

You might approach study of both Esther and Jonah by identifying their people, places, plot, and purpose. Ask these questions also: What do these stories tell us about the period between the testaments? What was happening to Judaism?

Review biblical history. Read in turn the dates and events in the chart of biblical history on page 126. As persons read the dates and events, they should pause to recall a particular person or event.

If persons did additional reading in Haggai, Zechariah, and Malachi, hear their reports. Or read portions of the books aloud.

BREAK

(10 minutes)

ENCOUNTER THE WORD

(40 minutes)

Scripture selection: Jonah 3:10–4:11

Read the story silently and work individually on these questions: What happened in this story? What did the story likely say to its first hearers? What did the writer of the story want to say for God? What is the story's central purpose? What does the story mean for me and my life? Talk in pairs. (See depth Bible study, pages 35–39 of *Teaching the Bible to Adults and Youth.*)

MARKS OF DISCIPLESHIP

(20 minutes)

Disciples hear the gospel of Jesus Christ in the context of unity with the historic people of God.

Read aloud "Our Human Condition." Talk about how the time between the testaments was a bridge, not a break. Discuss this question: What difference does it make to understanding the Bible when Christians see themselves as connected to the people of God through the Old Testament?

CLOSING AND PRAYER

(5 minutes)

Turn to Lesson 18 and write down prayer concerns. Close with prayer.

DISCIPLE

THE NEW TESTAMENT

18 Radical Discipleship

GATHERING AND PRAYER

(5 minutes)

VIDEO SEGMENT 18

(20 minutes)
Presenter: Michael J. Brown

Prepare to View Video
Listen for the major themes of Matthew and how these themes speak to its call for radical discipleship.

View Video
Summary of video content:
Five major themes in Matthew's portrait of Jesus:
- Jesus is a teacher. There is an emphasis on teaching throughout the Gospel and in the Great Commission
- Less emphasis is placed on miracles. Miracle stories introduce questions about discipleship.
- Jesus is the Jewish messiah, sent by a Jewish God, in fulfillment of the Jewish Scriptures.
- Emphasis is placed on a different kind of righteousness. A disciple's righteousness must be better, greater, more effective than the law requires.
- The Gospel's universal mission is found and cultivated in particular contexts.

Matthew's teaching calls for radical discipleship.

Discuss After Viewing Video
What are the major themes of Matthew? How does Matthew use these themes in its call for radical discipleship?

SCRIPTURE AND STUDY MANUAL

(50 minutes)
Establish the nature and purpose of the Gospel of Matthew by using information gathered in daily reading and from the introduction to Matthew in the Bible. Work in groups of three or four to answer these questions: Who wrote the book? When was it written? To whom? What are the major themes in the book? What point was the writer wanting to make about Jesus?

Call attention to the brief chart of dates on page 189 of the manual to get in mind the historical setting of the New Testament. Read dates and events in unison. Call out the dates and ask the group to respond with the events. Reverse the process.

An important question for this lesson is, What is radical or distinctive about the discipleship Jesus called for? Form four groups and assign a portion of the Sermon on the Mount to each group to begin answering the question: (1) Matthew 5:1-26; (2) Matthew 5:27–6:4; (3) Matthew 6:5-34; (4) Matthew 7:1-28. In the groups, work individually first, then together. Then hear a one-sentence summary from each group.

Work through daily notes with these questions: What do the notes say about radical discipleship? What does radical discipleship involve?

BREAK

(10 minutes)

ENCOUNTER THE WORD

(40 minutes)
Scripture selection: Matthew 20:1-16
Read Matthew 20:1-16 aloud while others follow in their Bibles. Ask everyone to read the passage silently. Work individually on these questions: What does this passage tell us about God? What does this passage tell us about human beings? What does this passage tell us about the relationship between God and human beings? Then discuss the questions in groups of three. (See theological Bible study, pages 40–44 of *Teaching the Bible to Adults and Youth.*)

MARKS OF DISCIPLESHIP

(20 minutes)
Disciples accept Christ's call to radical discipleship.
Share responses in this section to the extent persons are comfortable talking about where they are in their own discipleship. Discuss this question: Why does the church often settle for making church members instead of making disciples? The second question in this section of the study manual ties to "Our Human Condition." Read that statement aloud together and then respond to the question.

CLOSING AND PRAYER

(5 minutes)
Turn to Lesson 19 and write down prayer concerns. The assignment is a rereading of Matthew. Call attention to the special assignment on page 143. Close with prayer.

19 Mounting Controversy

GATHERING AND PRAYER

(5 minutes)

VIDEO SEGMENT 19

(20 minutes)
Presenter: Michael J. Brown

Prepare to View Video

Listen for the actions or events that point to Jesus' criticism of Jewish leadership.

View Video

Summary of video content:

In Matthew, the rejection of Jesus begins almost immediately. While the magi bring precious gifts to the child, Herod seeks to take his life. Jesus' birth evokes both acceptance and rejection the same as his death and resurrection and his deeds.

According to Matthew, the Pharisees are more concerned with proper observances of the Law than with helping others. Because of this, the Jewish leaders are portrayed as evil hypocrites. Opposition to Jesus and his criticism of the Jewish leaders builds.

- Jesus cleanses the Temple
- Jesus tells parables that portray his opponents in a negative way
- "Seven Woes" against the Pharisees

The problem for Jesus in Matthew is never the Jews or the Jewish religion. The problem is the Jewish leadership. Matthew affirms Judaism, but as it is interpreted by Jesus.

Discuss After Viewing Video

Discuss the tension between Jesus and the Jewish leadership. What does Jesus' criticism of the Jewish leadership say to those who would be his disciples?

SCRIPTURE AND STUDY MANUAL

(50 minutes)

The emphasis in this lesson is on value clashes, religious controversy, and political conflict. Form three groups. Ask one group to use their daily notes and the Scripture to identify and report value clashes. The second group, evidences of religious controversy; and the third group, evidences of political conflict.

The extent to which Jesus was and is a threat is apparent in Matthew 26–28. Look at events there from the standpoint of Matthew 16:24-25, the theme verse for this lesson. What is the nature of the cross we take up?

If we were comparing the religious groups of the first century with religious groups today, we would call them the pillars of the church. Discuss this question: How is Jesus at odds with the pillars of the church today?

BREAK

(10 minutes)

ENCOUNTER THE WORD

(40 minutes)

Scripture selection: Matthew 26:69-75

Ask everyone to read Matthew 26:69-75 silently. Then read the passage aloud while group members listen for sounds, smells, sights, tastes, and touches. With partners, list the different senses identified. Then imagine being in the courtyard that night. What would you be thinking and feeling? Tell your partner. (See using all the senses in Bible study, pages 57–61 of *Teaching the Bible to Adults and Youth.*)

MARKS OF DISCIPLESHIP

(20 minutes)

Disciples abandon sham and pretense, become vulnerable, and enter the ministry of making disciples.

Read "Our Human Condition" and the mark of discipleship. Jesus is a threat to us because his way calls for changing the way we live. How would becoming vulnerable affect the way of living described in "Our Human Condition"?

Discuss the responses members gave to the questions in the "Marks of Discipleship" section.

Note to the teacher: Plan together how group members will carry out the special assignment described at the end of the lesson.

CLOSING AND PRAYER

(5 minutes)

Turn to Lesson 20 and write down prayer concerns. Close with prayer.

20 The Hidden Messiah

GATHERING AND PRAYER

(5 minutes)

VIDEO SEGMENT 20

(20 minutes)
Presenter: Thomas E. Boomershine

Prepare to View Video
Listen for information about "the messianic secret."

View Video
Summary of video content:
Mark identifies Jesus as the Christ, the Son of God. *Christ* means Messiah in Hebrew, one who has been anointed. But Jesus was not the kind of Messiah people expected.

Throughout most of Mark's story, Jesus tries to keep his messianic identity secret. He tells those he healed to say nothing. He even tells his disciples to remain quiet. But the more Jesus said, "Keep quiet," the more people proclaimed his miraculous deeds.

It isn't until his trial before the Sanhedrin that Jesus makes his identity known and, when he does, he is condemned to death.

At the end of Mark the women who visited the empty tomb are told to go and tell. Yet, they say nothing to anyone. Were they afraid? We too are told to go and tell. What is our response?

Discuss After Viewing Video
Why did Jesus want to keep his identity secret? How would you describe the identity of Christ today? Now that the secret of Christ is out and we are called to tell the story, what is our response?

SCRIPTURE AND STUDY MANUAL

(50 minutes)
Hear special assignment reports (page 143).

Compare Matthew and Mark by seeing which stories and events are recorded in both books and which are unique to one or the other. Have group members use concordances or footnotes in their Bibles to find this information.

Draw on the information persons recorded in their daily notes to get a feeling for the tone of the Gospel of Mark as compared with the Gospel of Matthew. What gives Mark its sense of urgency?

Jesus ushered in the Kingdom by his acts of power. Discuss written responses on pages 147–49. Decide on some words that describe the kind of power Jesus demonstrated. Then ask each to respond to this question: What one question would you like to ask Jesus about his understanding of his power and the way he used it?

BREAK

(10 minutes)

ENCOUNTER THE WORD

(40 minutes)
Scripture selection: Mark 9:2-13

Ask one person to read Mark 9:2-13 aloud and others to follow in their Bibles. Involve the group in a mental drama. Use these statements and questions: Imagine yourself as Peter or James or John on the mountain with Jesus. What are you thinking and feeling as you watch what is happening? Imagine yourself as James or John. What do you think of Peter's suggestion? What are you wondering as you come down the mountain, especially when Jesus tells you not to tell anyone about your experience? Talk together about insights gained from this Scripture. (See personalized mental drama, pages 102–04 of *Teaching the Bible to Adults and Youth.*)

MARKS OF DISCIPLESHIP

(20 minutes)
Disciples understand their ministry as a call to self-denial and suffering.

Say the theme word together. Then read aloud the statement of "Our Human Condition." Discuss this question: How can suffering and self-denial be understood and experienced as good news? Then move to a discussion of the responses persons made to the questions in this section of the study manual.

Even if your group is not meeting during Lent, consider together the suggestion of fasting for one meal during the week and giving the money you save to buy food for hungry people.

CLOSING AND PRAYER

(5 minutes)
Turn to Lesson 21 and write down prayer concerns. Close with prayer.

21 God Seeks the Least, the Last, the Lost

GATHERING AND PRAYER

(5 minutes)

VIDEO SEGMENT 21

(20 minutes)
Presenter: R. Alan Culpepper

Prepare to View Video
Listen for what Luke wants readers to know about Jesus.

View Video
Summary of video content:
For Luke, Jesus was the Savior who had come to bring good news to the poor, release to the captives, and salvation to the lost. Beginning with the announcement of Jesus' birth, Luke weaves a story of one who came for all the least and the lost.

Luke demands that those who follow Jesus must do so in the dirty, violent world of hunger, disease, prejudice, and oppression. Discipleship is not just a matter of inward purity; it requires compassionate intervention on behalf of the poor, the hungry, the homeless, and the despised.

What was the sign that confirmed the Messiah had come? Jesus told John's followers to go back and tell him that "the blind see, the lame walk, the lepers are being cleansed, the deaf hear, the dead are being raised, and the poor hear good news."

Discuss After Viewing Video
What image of Jesus is portrayed in Luke? What kind of discipleship does Jesus call for in Luke?

SCRIPTURE AND STUDY MANUAL

(50 minutes)
Several parables are unique to Luke. To get a flavor of these parables, identify several and read them aloud. Use various reading techniques: responsive reading, reading in unison, one person reading while others listen, each person reading a verse in turn, dramatic reading with characters and a narrator. After the reading, invite persons to describe the messages they heard.

Use the theme verses (Luke 4:18-19) as a way of getting into Luke's emphasis on the least, the last, the lost. Assign teams of four persons to work through the Gospel of Luke and pick out incidents that illustrate Jesus' carrying out his mission as stated in the theme verses.

Invite teams to discuss the reasons persons are the least, the last, the lost. How did Jesus address each of these reasons?

BREAK

(10 minutes)

ENCOUNTER THE WORD

(40 minutes)
Scripture selection: Luke 16:19-31

Read Luke 16:19-31 aloud while others follow in their Bibles. Ask persons to say what they heard during this reading that they had not heard before.

Then in pairs or threes study the passage using these questions: What is the central idea of the passage? What meaning does this passage have for Christians today? What does this passage require of me? (See depth Bible study, pages 35–39 of *Teaching the Bible to Adults and Youth.*)

MARKS OF DISCIPLESHIP

(20 minutes)
Disciples throw their weight with God's mission to the least, the last, the lost.

In making the connection between the "Marks of Discipleship" and "Our Human Condition," begin by reading the statement of "Our Human Condition." Identify and discuss the stereotypes and attitudes of limited perspective in the statement. Invite persons to reflect silently on the tension they experience between the seduction of the comfortable, protected lifestyle and the demands of God's mission to the outcast.

Work through the questions in the study manual one at a time and then discuss this question: If we put ourselves into the position of the least, the last, and the lost, what do we need from Jesus?

CLOSING AND PRAYER

(5 minutes)
Turn to Lesson 22 and write down prayer concerns. Close with prayer.

22 Lifegiver

GATHERING AND PRAYER

(5 minutes)

VIDEO SEGMENT 22

(20 minutes)
Presenter: Jamie Clark-Soles

Prepare to View Video
Listen for the distinctive characteristics of the Gospel of John.

View Video
Summary of video content:
Distinctiveness of John's Gospel:
- no genealogy;
- no annunciation; no magi; no birth;
- begins before Creation;
- Jesus' ministry lasts three years;
- no parables; no exorcisms.

The Gospel of John emphasizes Jesus' power, sovereignty, glory, and divinity at every turn. Jesus is not baptized by John the Baptist. Jesus is not tempted in the wilderness. Jesus is not shown as a victim. Jesus is in control of everything.

The single message of John is that Jesus and God are one with each other and with all believers.

The Gospel of John could just as easily be called the Gospel of Life.

Unlike many New Testament writers, John indicates no belief whatsoever in hell. All judgment takes place in this life. John stresses repeatedly that the life Jesus promises is available now.

According to John, with Jesus you have all the life you need.

Discuss After Viewing Video
What are the distinctive characteristics of the Gospel of John? How does the Gospel of John describe the life believers can experience in Jesus Christ?

SCRIPTURE AND STUDY MANUAL

(50 minutes)
Using information persons gathered in their reading and study and from the notes they have made, work together to describe the Gospel of John. How does this Gospel differ from the other three in its tone, emphasis, and purpose? Why do you think many persons claim John as their favorite Gospel?

The symbols Jesus used to describe himself are life-sustaining. In pairs or threes, identify these symbols in the first twelve chapters of John and list the ways each symbol is life-sustaining. Invite some responses from the pairs or threes.

Read as little plays some encounters between people and Jesus in John's Gospel. Use one person to be John, the narrator. Here are two possibilities: Jesus and Nicodemus (3:1-21): Does Nicodemus remind you of anyone you know? Jesus, Mary, and Martha (11:1-53): Have you known people who found faith or "life" beside a grave?

Anticipate questions from group members on the relationship between suffering and sin. You may want to use a combination of total group and small group discussion on the subject.

BREAK

(10 minutes)

ENCOUNTER THE WORD

(40 minutes)
Scripture selection: John 10:7-18
Read John 10:7-18 aloud. Instruct group members to study the passage in groups of three and then individually rewrite it in their own words. Ask for volunteers to read their version to the entire group. (See paraphrasing, pages 71–76 of *Teaching the Bible to Adults and Youth.*)

Or study John 5:1-18 using the dialogue and encounter approach described on pages 51–56.

MARKS OF DISCIPLESHIP

(20 minutes)
Disciples experience life in Jesus Christ.
Read "Our Human Condition" aloud. Invite persons who would like to share their responses in the "Marks of Discipleship" section to do so. Compare the kind of life described in "Our Human Condition" with the life offered by Jesus Christ.

CLOSING AND PRAYER

(5 minutes)
Turn to Lesson 23 and write down prayer concerns. Close with prayer.

23 Advocate

GATHERING AND PRAYER

(5 minutes)

VIDEO SEGMENT 23

(20 minutes)
Presenter: Jamie Clark-Soles

Prepare to View Video

Listen for John's vision of the Holy Spirit and what makes it distinctive from the other Gospels.

View Video

Summary of video content:

In John, Jesus is the only person in the narrative who has a relationship with the Holy Spirit before the Crucifixion. No one else in the story receives the Holy Spirit until after Jesus is glorified through his crucifixion and resurrection.

Jesus establishes the future life of the believing community as the household of God. Through language of dwelling or abiding, Jesus speaks of relationship. Jesus comes and dwells among us and makes us children of God. God and Jesus dwell in one another; God, Jesus, and the Holy Spirit dwell in the believers.

Through the power of the Holy Spirit, the community of Jesus' disciples can carry out the only commandment given in the Gospel of John: Love one another.

Discuss After Viewing Video

Discuss the role of the Holy Spirit in the life of the believing community and in the life of the disciple.

SCRIPTURE AND STUDY MANUAL

(50 minutes)

Provide teams of three or four persons questions to guide their discussion of the assigned Scriptures. Four such questions are these: According to Jesus, what is to be the work of the Advocate? What promises does Jesus make to his disciples in his farewell to them? What commands does he give his disciples? What descriptions does Jesus give to his disciples of what is to come? The teams should draw upon their daily notes and the commentary in the study manual in answering the questions.

Chapters 18–21 of John contain many powerful scenes in the passion of Jesus. One of the following approaches might help persons hear the message in the Passion in a new way: (1) Read around the circle until you have read the entire account. (2) Tell one another the stories a scene at a time. (3) Let each member of the group choose and become one of the characters in the story and tell his or her part of the story from that character's point of view. The material may be broken up into these sections: John 18:1-11; 18:12-27; 18:28-40; 19:1-16; 19:17-30; 19:31-42; 20:1-18; 20:19-31; 21:1-14; 21:15-25. After any of these activities, take time to talk about what people felt as they listened and participated.

Before you complete your study of John, identify the ways John differs from the Synoptic Gospels, Matthew, Mark, and Luke.

BREAK

(10 minutes)

ENCOUNTER THE WORD

(40 minutes)

Scripture selection: John 13:1-20

Read aloud John 13:1-20 as others listen. In pairs identify the details and sequence of the story. Then ask persons to listen as you read it aloud for sounds, smells, sights, tastes, and touches. Still in pairs, list all the ways the story involved the senses. Discuss this question: What new understandings came from hearing the story this way? (See using all the senses in Bible study, pages 57–61 of *Teaching the Bible to Adults and Youth.*)

MARKS OF DISCIPLESHIP

(20 minutes)

Disciples sense the inner assurance of abundant, eternal life.

The theme word of the lesson, the statement of "Our Human Condition," and "Marks of Discipleship" are all tied together. Read "Our Human Condition" aloud. Then respond to the questions that are in the study manual under "Marks of Discipleship." Respect those persons who do not feel comfortable in talking about their personal experience.

CLOSING AND PRAYER

(5 minutes)

Turn to Lesson 24 and write down prayer concerns. Close with prayer.

24 The Explosive Power of the Spirit

GATHERING AND PRAYER

(5 minutes)

VIDEO SEGMENT 24

(20 minutes)
Presenter: Aida Besançon Spencer

Prepare to View Video

Listen for the source, means, and the purpose of the Holy Spirit's power.

View Video

Summary of video content:

The Book of the Acts of the Apostles describes a dynamic, explosive world where the Spirit of the risen Jesus is active.

The Spirit is active in proclaiming the name of Jesus, the source of its power; active through the prayers of believers, its means of power; and active in bearing witness to Jesus through preaching and healing, the purpose of its power.

Acts 1:8 sets the theme for the whole Book of Acts. Then Luke spends the rest of his narrative showing how Jesus' followers are empowered by the Holy Spirit as they witness to the Lord Jesus, even in the midst of opposition and conflict.

Discuss After Viewing Video

How did the early church experience the presence and power of the Holy Spirit? How do you experience the presence and power of the Holy Spirit in your life?

SCRIPTURE AND STUDY MANUAL

(50 minutes)

The theme word for this lesson is *power.* Work together to describe Holy Spirit power. Trace its effect on individuals and groups through this first part of Acts. How were persons' lives changed? How were their attitudes affected? What did they do with this power?

Acts is full of vibrant characters. Probe the first part of Acts by assigning a character to teams of two and ask them to walk with the character through the events in which the character is involved. They should try to sense the excitement, power, feelings, and reactions of the character as the events unfolded. Allow time for the teams to talk to the group about what they discovered.

The whole of Israel's history comes into play more than once in Acts. Try to identify what was at stake for these early Christians, Jews within Judaism, claimed by their history, but committed to the message and mission of Jesus. What tensions with fellow Jews were built into that situation?

Have maps available or have persons use the maps in their Bibles to trace the movement of Christianity into the Gentile world. Work in teams of two to scan the daily blocks of Scripture for the points at which early Christianity moved out of Judaism and into the Gentile world. Look for boundaries crossed both in events and attitudes.

BREAK

(10 minutes)

ENCOUNTER THE WORD

(40 minutes)

Scripture selection: Acts 4:32–5:11

Ask everyone to read Acts 4:32–5:11 silently and then listen as one person reads it aloud. In threes, study the passage, using these questions: What does this passage say about God? What does this passage say about human beings? What does this passage say about the relationship between God and human beings? (See theological Bible study, pages 40–44 of *Teaching the Bible to Adults and Youth.*)

MARKS OF DISCIPLESHIP

(20 minutes)

Disciples experience the presence and the power of the Holy Spirit in their life.

The connection between the mark of discipleship for this lesson and "Our Human Condition" lies in the importance of waiting and praying for the power that comes with the baptism of the Holy Spirit. Discuss responses persons have written to the questions in "Marks of Discipleship."

CLOSING AND PRAYER

(5 minutes)

Turn to Lesson 25 and write down prayer concerns. Close with prayer.

25 The Gospel Penetrates the World

GATHERING AND PRAYER

(5 minutes)

VIDEO SEGMENT 25

(20 minutes)
Presenter: Aida Besançon Spencer

Prepare to View Video

Listen for the strategies the early Christians used to carry out their mission to spread the gospel.

View Video

Summary of video content:

Acts is the story of those who first proclaimed the story of Jesus. In spite of difficulties, the earliest Christians developed particular strategies for accomplishing their mission to spread the gospel: using missionary teams to spread the gospel and accepting hospitality as an entry point for sharing the gospel.

The missionary teams prepared the way for sharing the gospel, sustained new communities of believers, and followed up with believers previously visited.

Learning to manage differences in language, ethnicity, even theological belief, the early church in Acts took seriously the task of proclaiming Christ to the ends of the earth.

Discuss After Viewing Video

What are your thoughts about the strategies used by the early Christians to spread the gospel? What do these strategies teach about how to spread the gospel today?

SCRIPTURE AND STUDY MANUAL

(50 minutes)

The accounts of the second and third missionary journeys are in Acts 15:36–18:23 and 18:24–21:14. Trace the two journeys through the Scripture, paying particular attention to the key stops along the way, the events that took place at those stops, Paul's purpose for and the outcome of his visit to a particular location, and the journey itself. Group members should use their notes as well as the Scripture reporting the journeys.

The sequence and nature of the events reported in Acts 21:15–28:31 are fairly complicated. Use these questions to clarify the information: What were the events, and what was their sequence? What were the issues related to the events? What were the outcomes of the events in terms of their impact on the spread of the gospel?

Paul is the central character in the latter part of Acts. Construct a portrait of Paul from the reading and study persons have done during the week and from the discussion in the group meeting. Describe Paul the man, Paul the Jew, Paul the missionary, and Paul's motivation and message. Then discuss this question in pairs or threes: In what ways does Paul serve as a model for you in your role as a disciple?

BREAK

(10 minutes)

ENCOUNTER THE WORD

(40 minutes)

Scripture selection: Ephesians 1:3–2:10

Read Ephesians 1:3–2:10 aloud with each person reading a few verses. Work on the passage individually and then in groups of three to discuss these questions: What does this passage tell us about God? What does this passage tell us about human beings? What does this passage tell us about the relationship between God and human beings? (See theological Bible study, pages 40–44 of *Teaching the Bible to Adults and Youth.*)

MARKS OF DISCIPLESHIP

(20 minutes)

Disciples witness to others in order to lead them to Jesus Christ.

Talk about whether the statement of "Our Human Condition" is an accurate description of persons' experience. How can we overcome our hesitancy to witness to others about Jesus Christ? Invite volunteers to share what they have written in the study manual under "Marks of Discipleship."

CLOSING AND PRAYER

(5 minutes)

Turn to Lesson 26 and write down prayer concerns. Close with prayer.

26 Put Right With God Through Faith

GATHERING AND PRAYER

(5 minutes)

VIDEO SEGMENT 26

(20 minutes)
Presenter: Richard B. Hays

Prepare to View Video
Listen for reasons Romans raises the question, "Can God be trusted?" and how Paul answers it.

View Video
Summary of video content:
The key question that drives the whole letter of Romans is this: Can God be trusted?

Paul addresses the problem of God's universal justice, God's faithfulness to Israel, and how the death and resurrection of Jesus are to be understood as the fulfillment, rather than the undoing, of all that God has promised Israel from the beginning.

Why did he send this letter to Rome?

- Roman Christians needed to hear that the real Lord—the real giver of peace, justice, and salvation—was Jesus, not Caesar.
- Paul was also writing to appeal for support as he continued his missionary journeys.

Paul's letter to the Romans confirms that the God who has chosen us freely in love can be trusted.

Discuss After Viewing Video
What points does Paul make in arguing that God can be trusted? Why is the question, "Can God be trusted?" so crucial for Paul? How is that question still crucial for Christians?

SCRIPTURE AND STUDY MANUAL

(50 minutes)
Work together to compile a list of theological ideas from Romans that can become a statement of the gospel message for the members of the group. This procedure will require scanning blocks of Scripture. Then work in pairs to develop a written creed or statement of faith from the ideas listed by the entire group. Ask each pair to read their statement aloud.

Some discussion may center on the restoration of Israel. Before such a discussion, read aloud and straight through Chapters 9–11. Then go back and look at the chapters one at a time, inviting persons to comment or raise questions for further discussion. After working through the three chapters in this fashion, read the section in the study manual on the restoration of Israel for further discussion. One important understanding to be grasped is our (Gentile Christians) role as "a wild olive shoot" grafted into the "olive tree." What does that mean?

BREAK

(10 minutes)

ENCOUNTER THE WORD

(40 minutes)
Scripture selection: Romans 4:13–5:5

Have two persons read aloud Romans 4:13–5:5, the first reading 4:13-22 and the second reading 4:23–5:5. Ask others to follow in their Bibles. Study the passage in pairs, using these questions: What does this passage tell us about God? What does this passage tell us about human beings? What does this passage tell us about the relationship between God and human beings? (See theological Bible study, pages 40–44 of *Teaching the Bible to Adults and Youth.*)

MARKS OF DISCIPLESHIP

(20 minutes)
Disciples receive and trust the forgiving love of God in Jesus Christ and serve out of love and gratitude.

Read aloud "Our Human Condition." Talk about whether it accurately describes persons' experience. How does an attitude of accepting and trusting relate to the situation described in "Our Human Condition"? Make use of what persons have written in the study manual under "Marks of Discipleship."

Note to the teacher: At the beginning of your study of Paul's letters, call attention to page 197 in the study manual. Suggest that persons work on it during the next few weeks and that you will come back to it after Lesson 29.

CLOSING AND PRAYER

(5 minutes)
Turn to Lesson 27 and write down prayer concerns. Close with prayer.

27 A Congregation in Ferment

GATHERING AND PRAYER

(5 minutes)

VIDEO SEGMENT 27

(20 minutes)
Presenter: Gay L. Byron

Prepare to View Video

Listen for the issues facing the Corinthians and Paul's message to them.

View Video

Summary of video content:

Paul's first letter to the Corinthians is in response to questions he had received from various leaders in the community regarding: divisions in the community, sexual immorality, lawsuits, and the Lord's supper.

The main point of Paul's first letter to the Corinthians can be summed up when he says, "all of you be in agreement . . . be united in the same mind and the same purpose."

Central to Paul's teachings to this community was the cross and the resurrection of Christ.

Paul identifies what is crucial to the church then and today: the unity of the Body.

Discuss After Viewing Video

What were the issues facing the Corinthian congregation? What was Paul's message? How is the message of Corinthians relevant to the church today?

SCRIPTURE AND STUDY MANUAL

(50 minutes)

If persons in the group did research on ancient Corinth, hear their reports first.

Though the Corinthian letters concern the affairs of a first-century church, they are concerns familiar to us. Divide the week's Scripture assignments among groups of three for study, using these questions: What were some of the concerns of the Corinthian church? What advice did Paul give? What concerns face our local church today? How might the advice Paul gave to the Corinthians be useful to our church? Put the questions on newsprint for all to see.

We get three main pictures in the Corinthian letters: a picture of Paul, a picture of the gospel message, and a picture of a first-century local church. What is in each picture? To answer that question, form three teams and assign each team the task of creating one of the pictures. The teams might choose to present their picture through words, actions, drawings, music, or another form.

The theme word for this lesson is *love.* Why is that word so important to the Corinthian church and to the modern local church?

Though 1 Corinthians 13 and 15 are both familiar passages to most Christians, hearing them read is always a powerful experience. Read them aloud in unison, as a responsive reading, or with one person reading aloud and others listening. Follow the reading with these questions: What did you hear? What did you wonder? What did you feel?

BREAK

(10 minutes)

ENCOUNTER THE WORD

(40 minutes)

Scripture selection: 1 Corinthians 10:1-13 or 3:1-23

Ask someone to read the passage aloud while others follow in their Bibles. Then ask persons to rewrite the passage in their own words. Invite volunteers to read aloud what they have written. (See paraphrasing, pages 71–76 of *Teaching the Bible to Adults and Youth.*)

MARKS OF DISCIPLESHIP

(20 minutes)

Disciples love.

Love is both the theme word and the mark of discipleship for this lesson. How does showing love relate to "Our Human Condition"?

Decide which of the questions in "Marks of Discipleship" are appropriate for open discussion. By this time the trust level in the group may be high enough for open discussion of personal questions.

CLOSING AND PRAYER

(5 minutes)

Turn to Lesson 28 and write down prayer concerns. Close with prayer.

28 The Son Shall Set Us Free

GATHERING AND PRAYER

(5 minutes)

VIDEO SEGMENT 28

(20 minutes)
Presenter: Brad R. Braxton

Prepare to View Video

Listen for the religious and social boundaries of the church that are addressed in Galatians.

View Video

Summary of video content:

Galatians is an impassioned conversation about the religious and social boundaries of the church.

Paul insisted that faith in Christ did not obligate Gentiles to convert to Judaism. Following the Law did not bring justification or a proper relationship with God. This is possible through faith alone.

Justification by faith is not simply about individual salvation, regardless of social differences. It also allows the church to express communal unity in the midst of social diversity. Paul pleads for the erasure of dominance, not the removal of difference.

Christian faith not only engenders communal harmony, but also freedom. Believers have been freed from enslaving forces and freed for loving service to the neighbor.

Discuss After Viewing Video

What is the freedom that the Christian faith engenders? To what extent does your church express communal unity in the midst of social diversity?

SCRIPTURE AND STUDY MANUAL

(50 minutes)

Provide teams of three with sheets of newsprint and marking pens and ask them to write in their own words a statement of the issue central to Galatians. No doubt each group will state the issue a little differently. Read the finished statements one at a time and ask for questions for clarification.

Consider and discuss the following issues one at a time with group members providing thoughts and information from their daily reading and study: circumcision, law of Moses, Jerusalem Council, justification by faith alone, Abraham and the Law, Abraham and Christ, Hellenism, Judaizers, Gentile Christians, Jewish Christians, Paul and his history.

What was Paul's main point? What was the point of the opponents? If Paul had surrendered his point, what would have been the outcome?

Have small groups talk about their own experiences of trying to live by a religion of "rules." Use responses on pages 211–12. Then ask them to say whether they are now experiencing a freedom from living by rules in their relationship with God. If so, how did they gain freedom? If not, what is keeping them from experiencing such freedom? What does Jesus Christ set us free to do?

BREAK

(10 minutes)

ENCOUNTER THE WORD

(40 minutes)

Scripture selection: Galatians 5:1–6:10

Ask one person to read aloud Galatians 5:1-26 and another to read 6:1-10 while others follow along in their Bibles. Then in threes discuss these questions: What does this passage tell us about God? What does this passage tell us about human beings? What does this passage tell us about the relationship between God and human beings? (See theological Bible study, pages 40–44 of *Teaching the Bible to Adults and Youth.*)

MARKS OF DISCIPLESHIP

(20 minutes)

Disciples experience and express freedom as loving God and loving neighbor.

Read aloud "Our Human Condition." Talk about times when persons felt exactly what the statement describes. What is the message in Galatians to the situation described in "Our Human Condition"? Work first in teams and then as a total group on the second question under "Marks of Discipleship." The last question in this section focuses the issue on the congregation, making it appropriate for open discussion in the group.

CLOSING AND PRAYER

(5 minutes)

Turn to Lesson 29 and write down prayer concerns. Close with prayer.

29 A Pastor Gives Guidance

GATHERING AND PRAYER

(5 minutes)

VIDEO SEGMENT 29

(20 minutes)
Presenter: Minerva G. Carcaño

Prepare to View Video
Listen for the advice given to Timothy and Titus.

View Video
Summary of video content:
The Pastoral Letters are written as pastoral advice to Timothy and Titus.
Challenges facing the church: false teachings and church leadership.
The church is called to live together as a family.
Characteristics of good leadership: each leader has a particular function and all functions are equal; each leader is to faithfully proclaim, through word and deed, "sound teaching."
What is important to teach and preach? One God; call of Christians to be the "household of God"; desire of God for all to be saved; sound doctrine.
Christian leaders are to model godly living so their sisters and brothers in the household of God can learn to do the same.

Discuss After Viewing Video
What challenges faced the church described in Timothy and Titus? What advice did Paul give? What challenges confront Christians trying to live together as family in today's world?

SCRIPTURE AND STUDY MANUAL

(50 minutes)
Organize the discussion around the five main points of Paul's counsel to Timothy discussed in the study manual. Working in twos or threes with Bibles and notes from daily reading and study, summarize what Paul said about (1) helping people adhere to the central doctrines of the faith, (2) teaching diligently, (3) respecting spiritual authority and leadership, (4) caring for family, and (5) handling money. How do these issues concern us today? Use written responses from pages 218–19.

Identify the central doctrines of the faith according to the letters to Timothy and Titus. See, for example, Titus 1:1-3; 2:11-14; 3:4-7. Scan the letters for other similar statements of doctrine.

If group members prepared reports on Titus, hear them one at a time or perhaps as a panel.

Since this is the last of the letters of Paul that you will be studying, this would be a good time to go back to page 197 of the study manual and work in teams to complete it. Or if persons have already completed it, hear what they discovered.

BREAK

(10 minutes)

ENCOUNTER THE WORD

(40 minutes)
Scripture selection: 1 Timothy 6:3-20
Have someone read 1 Timothy 6:3-20 while others follow in their Bibles. Ask all persons to write down insights they received from the Scripture. For each of the next three steps, work individually and then with a partner. Find a different partner for each step. (1) Write down the central idea of the passage. (2) Write down the meaning the passage has for today's world. (3) Write down the personal meaning in the passage. (See depth Bible study, pages 35–39 of *Teaching the Bible to Adults and Youth.*)

MARKS OF DISCIPLESHIP

(20 minutes)
Disciples seek sound teaching under the guidance of faithful leaders.
Read aloud "Our Human Condition" and the mark of discipleship. Discuss how respect for leaders who give guidance and the desire to discover things for oneself can work together rather than against each other. Then discuss the first question in the study manual under "Marks of Discipleship."

While persons might hesitate to tell what guidelines they have written for their attitudes toward money, they might be willing to talk about the questions they had to consider before writing their guidelines.

CLOSING AND PRAYER

(5 minutes)
Turn to Lesson 30 and write down prayer concerns. Close with prayer.

30 Our Great High Priest

GATHERING AND PRAYER

(5 minutes)

VIDEO SEGMENT 30

(20 minutes)
Presenter: David A. deSilva

Prepare to View Video
Listen for the message of Hebrews and note the importance the image of high priest plays in the message.

View Video
Summary of video content:
Hebrews shows how Jesus is the culmination of the hope of God's people expressed and foreshadowed throughout Scripture.

Subjected to persecution for their association with Jesus, the believers addressed in Hebrews have begun to doubt that the gifts and promises they have received in Jesus are worth the cost and have begun to slip away from association with the church.

The writer of Hebrews hopes to correct this perspective and mobilize the community to help one another persevere in faith and gratitude toward God and Jesus and to enable a faithful response to each new challenge of discipleship.

Discuss After Viewing Video
What is the message of Hebrews and what does it teach about Christian discipleship?

SCRIPTURE AND STUDY MANUAL

(50 minutes)
The central point for discussion is the superiority of Jesus Christ. Identify the arguments made by the writer of Hebrews for the superiority of Jesus. Ask persons to read aloud related verses or phrases from their Bibles.

Hebrews speaks to the problem of weakening faith. Locate Scriptures describing evidence of fading faith. Then discuss this question: How does the response made by Hebrews to the problem provide the necessary endurance and patience?

Many persons may have difficulty finding meaning in Hebrews. Two questions might help: What strength do you draw from the knowledge that Jesus faced the same temptations we face? What does Jesus' sacrifice mean for the way you live?

Much is said in Hebrews about the similarities and differences between the first covenant and the new covenant. Using information persons have written in their study manual and other information they can identify, make two lists—one of similarities and the other of differences in the first covenant and the new covenant. How do these similarities or differences contribute to the teaching of the superiority of Jesus Christ?

Stand and read responsively Hebrews 11–13 as an exhortation to one another to remain faithful.

BREAK

(10 minutes)

ENCOUNTER THE WORD

(40 minutes)
Scripture selection: Hebrews 4:14–5:14
Read Hebrews 4:14–5:14 aloud. Then, working individually, write down (1) new insights from the Scripture, (2) the central idea of the Scripture, (3) the meaning of the Scripture for today's world, (4) the personal meaning of the Scripture. Discuss each item in pairs. (See depth Bible study, pages 35–39 of *Teaching the Bible to Adults and Youth.*)

MARKS OF DISCIPLESHIP

(20 minutes)
Disciples accept God's forgiveness.
Read "Our Human Condition" aloud. Then ask this question: What power do sacrifice and forgiveness have for the condition described there?

One way to encourage persons to talk about the responses they have written in the study manual in this section would be for you to read your responses first. Some persons may decline, and others may prefer to discuss their responses in small groups rather than in the total group.

CLOSING AND PRAYER

(5 minutes)
Turn to Lesson 31 and write down prayer concerns. Sing one of the songs under "If You Want to Know More."

31 A People Set Apart

GATHERING AND PRAYER

(5 minutes)

VIDEO SEGMENT 31

(20 minutes)
Presenter: Leticia Guardiola-Sáenz

Prepare to View Video

Listen for what it means to be a people set apart, priests in the service of God.

View Video

Summary of video content:

The books of First and Second Peter deliver a particular message for a particular people. These people have been "chosen and destined" for God and are living scattered among strangers. They are "a chosen race, a royal priesthood, a holy nation, God's own people."

Even in the midst of the trials and tribulations they are suffering, God has not abandoned them; they are still God's own people.

The role of priests in ancient Israel was to serve as intermediaries between God and Israel. They were devoted to reconciling people with God.

The tribe of the Levites was the only tribe that did not receive territory in the Promised Land. They were scattered among the rest of the tribes of Israel.

Like the Levite priests, the role of Israel was to be a nation set apart, a kingdom of priests and a holy nation, to proclaim God's purpose to the nations.

Discuss After Viewing Video

What did it mean to be a people set apart to proclaim God's purpose to the nations for first-century Christians? What does it mean for Christians in the twenty-first century?

SCRIPTURE AND STUDY MANUAL

(50 minutes)

Some of the themes in this lesson are these: an emphasis on new creation in Christ, the meaning of *holy,* the experience of being set apart, the suffering that results from holy living or from being set apart.

Work on the following assignment in pairs, using the Bible and notes from daily reading and study: According to First and Second Peter, what are some ways disciples are set apart? What kind of suffering results from holy living or being set apart? Write a definition of "holy living" and read it in the total group.

Work on each question in "The Bible Teaching" in this way: First share responses in threes; then talk about responses in the total group.

BREAK

(10 minutes)

ENCOUNTER THE WORD

(40 minutes)

Scripture selection: 1 Peter 3:8-17

Ask someone to read aloud 1 Peter 3:8-17. Ask all persons to put into their own words what the passage says about being holy or set apart. Then with partners reread 1 Peter 3:15 and take turns saying what answer you would give to explain the hope you have in you. (See paraphrasing, pages 71–76 of *Teaching the Bible to Adults and Youth.*)

MARKS OF DISCIPLESHIP

(20 minutes)

Disciples know themselves as distinctive, peculiar people bearing the inner mark of character and the outer mark of compassion.

Read aloud "Our Human Condition" and ask persons to identify those sentences in the statement that have at some time expressed their feelings. Take a few minutes to list positive and negative understandings of the word *holy.* Discuss this question: Do we tend to interpret *holy* in a negative sense more often than in a positive sense? If so, why?

Ask for volunteers to read the first paragraph they have written under "Marks of Discipleship." Read in turn the second paragraph called for and discuss as a total group.

What is it that keeps the person described under "Marks of Discipleship" from being the person described in "Our Human Condition"?

CLOSING AND PRAYER

(5 minutes)

Turn to Lesson 32 and write down prayer concerns. Close with prayer.

32 We Never Lose Hope

GATHERING AND PRAYER

(5 minutes)

VIDEO SEGMENT 32

(20 minutes)
Presenter: Craig C. Hill

Prepare to View Video
Listen for the characteristics of apocalyptic writing and the message of the Book of Revelation.

View Video
Summary of video content:
Most scholars regard the Book of Revelation, an apocalyptic writing, as a book of theological insight.
An apocalypse is an "unveiling" or "revelation" of the true nature of reality.
An apocalypse was written during times of severe trial as a way of encouraging believers.
The message is often conveyed through mysterious images and cryptic language.
Each of the key apocalyptic concepts—for example, the judgment and rebirth of creation—says something important about the character of God, which is the essential subject of apocalyptic literature.
The conclusion of Revelation describes a reality in which apocalyptic disclosure is unnecessary. God is no longer distant, in heaven and in secret, but is instead on earth, present and known.
Revelation offers us a theology of creation's completion. No power or principality, no injustice or evil, will thwart God's good purpose.

Discuss After Viewing Video
What is the essential subject of apocalyptic writing? What does it mean to say that Revelation offers a theology of creation's completion?

SCRIPTURE AND STUDY MANUAL

(50 minutes)
As you prepare to teach, go back to the lesson on Daniel to review the themes and characteristics of apocalyptic literature. Put this information on newsprint to see during discussion.
Form five groups and assign each group one of these Scriptures: Revelation 1:4–3:22; 4–7; 8–12; 17–20; 21–22. Ask the groups to study the Scriptures and answer these questions: Where in the symbolic language do you hear the message of hope and encouragement to remain faithful? What meaning might this Scripture have for us today?
Divide the chart of biblical history on page 242 among teams of two to recall a memory related to the people or events. Then in the whole group read the dates and events, pausing for assigned teams to mention one related memory.
The themes and images of Revelation have been woven into hymns and other musical compositions. Sing some of the great hymns, especially "Holy, Holy, Holy!" or "Crown Him With Many Crowns." Read "Lo, He Comes With Clouds Descending."

BREAK

(10 minutes)

ENCOUNTER THE WORD

(40 minutes)
Scripture selection: Revelation 21:22–22:5
Read Revelation 21:22–22:5 in unison. Then ask the group to listen with their eyes closed as you read it aloud for sounds, sights, smells, touches, and tastes. With partners, talk about which senses the Scripture appealed to and describe to each other personal feelings while hearing the Scripture. Describe the hope that comes through this passage. (See using all the senses in Bible study, pages 57–61 of *Teaching the Bible to Adults and Youth.*)

MARKS OF DISCIPLESHIP

(20 minutes)
Disciples remain faithful to God in the midst of persecution and suffering.
Read the statement of "Our Human Condition." Ask persons what answer they give themselves and what answer they would give anyone who asks them, Where is the victory? Where is the hope?
Respond to the questions in the study manual under "Marks of Discipleship" in the whole group or in teams. Then read aloud the mark of discipleship.

CLOSING AND PRAYER

(5 minutes)
Turn to Lesson 33 and write down prayer concerns. Call attention to the preparation necessary for the next meeting. Close with prayer.

33 Gifts of Each Disciple

Note to the teacher: This lesson will differ in content and sequence from earlier ones. Emphasis here will be on ministry, service, servanthood. Be prepared to suggest areas of ministry within the congregation. Have a plan ready for helping persons move into places of service and be supported as they serve.

Disciples use their gifts in ministry to others.

GATHERING AND PRAYER

(5 minutes)

VIDEO SEGMENT 33

(20 minutes)
Presenter: John S. Mogabgab

Prepare to View Video

This segment presents the image of one's journey toward God as a means of preparing the group for decisions they will make as individuals and as a group about doing God's Word and becoming God's presence following the completion of their study of DISCIPLE.

View Video

Summary of video content:

God continues to desire our companionship. It is a call that echoes all the way from Genesis to the Book of Revelation.

Not content to be near us, God unbelievably decides to become one of us and one with us in struggle and hope.

To be truly fulfilled, a reciprocal movement from our side must meet God's movement toward us in Jesus Christ. This journey toward God involves the following: choosing God's way, receiving God's gifts, doing God's Word, and becoming God's presence.

By the power of love at work in us, God can do infinitely more than we can ask or even imagine.

Discuss After Viewing Video

Invite group members to talk in pairs about the thoughts and feelings they had as they watched this video. Then discuss this question: What does it mean to become God's presence in the world today?

CONSULTATION ON GIFTS

(2 hours)

Select a portion of each of the assigned daily Scriptures for reading aloud. The reading may vary, sometimes with the group reading together, sometimes with an individual reading. Then ask persons to talk briefly in pairs about the response they made in the manual relating to that Scripture. Have pairs change partners for describing responses to each of the Scripture readings.

Move then into a discussion of each person's gifts for ministry. Begin by briefly going around the group and asking all persons to say what they learned about themselves as they worked through the Scripture and the study manual during the week. Limit each person to one minute.

Express support to one another by having the members of the group tell each individual in the group all of the positive images they have of that person. Plan five minutes per person, including the teacher. Start with the first person; let every other member in the group say what he or she wishes to say to that person. Then have a brief prayer for guidance in relation to that person's choice of ministry. Follow this procedure for each person in the group until all thirteen group members have received the positive comments of the entire group and have had a prayer prayed for each of them.

After a break, work through the section of the study manual that deals with the seven gifts. Discuss each person's thinking about members' gifts for ministry, move toward consensus about each person's gifts, and record the agreements on page 249 of the study manual. After all persons have made their decisions about their commitments, let each person in turn tell the group what her or his commitment is. Follow this sharing with prayer.

Determine how these decisions for ministry will be communicated to members of the congregation who can help persons match their commitment with an opportunity for service.

CLOSING AND PRAYER

(5 minutes)

Look ahead to Lesson 34. Decide who from the group will read the Scripture selections in the Covenant Service and who will assist in serving the elements. Close with prayer.

34 A Last Supper Together

Note to the teacher: This group meeting will be different in sequence and content from earlier meetings. Before the meeting, make the necessary arrangements for Holy Communion. If you are not an ordained minister or if there is not an ordained minister in the group, invite an ordained minister to attend this meeting to administer the sacrament of Holy Communion.

GATHERING AND PRAYER

(5 minutes)

SCRIPTURE AND STUDY MANUAL

(50 minutes)

Pick up on three words from the study manual as a focus for your work in this time: *covenant, communion,* and *commitment.* First, ask persons to think back over their reading of Scripture and the study manual to complete this statement: *We are covenant people united to Abraham and Sarah, and these are ways we experience that covenant: . . .* Give persons time to complete the statement individually. Again, recalling Scripture and the study manual, complete this statement: *We are new covenant people united to Jesus Christ, and these are ways we experience that covenant: . . .* After all have completed this statement, let persons read in turn their first statement. Do the same with the second statement.

In exploring the subject of commitment, have the group identify passages from the Sermon on the Mount as examples of the committed life.

The mark of discipleship for this lesson is about commitment: *Disciples commit their life completely to God to serve as God wills.* Invite group members to describe the difference between the life of commitment and the life of neglect that is reflected in "Our Human Condition."

Remember is the theme word for this lesson, and most of the activities focus on remembering. This would be an appropriate place to have persons talk about the memories they recorded on page 243.

ENCOUNTER THE WORD

(40 minutes)

Scripture selection: 2 Corinthians 3:2-6

Read or have someone read aloud 2 Corinthians 3:2-6. Individually paraphrase the passage. Invite persons to read what they have written. (See paraphrasing, pages 71–76 of *Teaching the Bible to Adults and Youth.*)

BREAK

(10 minutes)

VIDEO SEGMENT 34

(20 minutes)
Presenter: Zan W. Holmes, Jr.

Prepare to View Video

The video segment will prepare the group for the Covenant Service. After viewing the video, move into the service without discussion.

View Video

Summary of video content:

The Bible talks about a covenant as an agreement between God and God's people.

The new covenant affirms that the "heart of the problem is the problem of the heart." God thus promises to change the people from the inside out. What God's people cannot do for themselves, God will do for them, in an act of pure mercy and love.

The making of the new covenant with God is not an individual act. It is a communal one. It is the work of the community of faith.

The covenant involves not only obligations toward God, but also obligations toward the members of the community. So as members of the new covenant community, let us remind ourselves that we can love because we are loved.

COVENANT SERVICE

(30 minutes)

Make all arrangements ahead of time for persons who will have special responsibility in the Covenant Service. Have hymnals or song sheets available for the songs used in the service.

The Dismissal with Blessing at the end of the service will bring to a close your study of DISCIPLE.

LOVE FEAST

(30 minutes)

Celebrating the bond among you by sharing time and food together would be appropriate either before or after the group meeting.

Second Edition (1993) Video Segments

On pages 51–54 you will find information and suggestions for using the Second Edition (1993) Video Segments. This earlier version of videos is not included in the Second Edition Revised 2005 Video Segments. To be sure which videos you are using, look for the Revised 2005 banner across the front of either the VHS or DVD case. If there is no banner, then you have the Second Edition (1993) version and should follow the suggestions below for the group meetings.

VIDEO SEGMENT 1

Presenters: Albert C. Outler, Richard B. Wilke

Prepare to View Video

Listen and take notes on what is said about the Bible, about God, and about the relationship between God and human beings.

Discuss After Viewing Video

What did you hear about the Bible? about God? about the relationship between God and human beings?

VIDEO SEGMENT 2

Presenter: B. Davie Napier

Prepare to View Video

Listen for three main points: the theological nature of the Creation story, how the Creation story became Creation faith, and how the two Creation accounts together express Israel's Creation faith.

Discuss After Viewing Video

What does it mean to think of the Creation story as theological rather than historical or scientific? What do you understand to be the difference between the Creation story and Creation faith?

VIDEO SEGMENT 3

Presenter: William Power

Prepare to View Video

Listen to a familiar story for new insights about who we are and who God is.

Discuss After Viewing Video

What new ideas did you hear about human beings and about their need of God and others? The word *sin* is not used in the story. How does the idea of sin apply here?

VIDEO SEGMENT 4

Presenter: Randall M. Falk

Prepare to View Video

God's call and God's covenant always go together. Invite persons to listen and watch for connections between the call and the covenant.

Discuss After Viewing Video

What relationship do you see between God's call and God's covenant?

VIDEO SEGMENT 5

Presenter: Randall M. Falk

Prepare to View Video

Introduce Passover as a time of joy and gratitude for Jews. Listen for what Jews are celebrating in Passover.

Discuss After Viewing Video

What are Jews celebrating in Passover? Why do they feel joy and gratitude? How would you compare the feelings you have during Holy Communion?

VIDEO SEGMENT 6

Presenter: Walter J. Harrelson

Prepare to View Video

Before viewing this video segment, read Exodus 20:1-17 aloud together. Ask the group to listen for explanation of the groupings of the commandments and of the value in their negative phrasing.

Discuss After Viewing Video

What is lost if the negative commandment is stated positively? Try restating all the commandments positively.

VIDEO SEGMENT 7

Presenter: Bernhard W. Anderson

Prepare to View Video

Listen and take notes on what is expressed and what is accomplished in making sacrifices to God.

Discuss After Viewing Video

Why were sacrifices necessary? What was the meaning of the sacrifices for the relationship between God and people?

VIDEO SEGMENT 8

Presenters: Albert C. Outler, Richard B. Wilke

Prepare to View Video

Listen with these questions in mind: Who were the judges and why were they necessary? How are we to understand the violence and bloodshed in these accounts?

Discuss After Viewing Video

Discuss the questions suggested above.

VIDEO SEGMENT 9

Presenter: Kathleen A. Farmer

Prepare to View Video

Listen for why the people wanted a king and what happened when God gave them what they wanted.

Discuss After Viewing Video

What was the people's experience of a king? How do you think the experience of exile influenced what appears in the books of Samuel?

VIDEO SEGMENT 10

Presenter: B. Davie Napier

Prepare to View Video

Ask viewers to put themselves into two opposing roles as they listen: the role of the prophet-minister and the role of royalty to whom the prophet-minister speaks.

Discuss After Viewing Video

In what sense are corruption of worship of God by pagan practices and social injustice still issues to which prophets must speak?

VIDEO SEGMENT 11

Presenter: B. Davie Napier

Prepare to View Video

Again we listen from two perspectives—that of Jeremiah and his role as prophet and that of being Jeremiah with the word of God to proclaim.

Discuss After Viewing Video

What was the word Jeremiah was called to speak? What needed reforming? How do you think it felt to be Jeremiah?

VIDEO SEGMENT 12

Presenter: Walter Brueggemann

Prepare to View Video

Listen for the effect of exile and the three biblical responses to the crisis of the exile.

Discuss After Viewing Video

Describe the situation of the people of Judah in 587 B.C.E. What is surprising about the three responses to the crisis of exile?

VIDEO SEGMENT 13

Presenter: Walter J. Harrelson

Prepare to View Video

Listen for what the Psalms have to offer us and for ways to use the Psalms.

Discuss After Viewing Video

Why do we often turn to the Psalms? What are some ways we can use the Psalms?

VIDEO SEGMENT 14

Presenters: Albert C. Outler, Richard B. Wilke

Prepare to View Video

Encourage viewers to visualize a people returning from exile.

Discuss After Viewing Video

Describe the reconstituted covenant community. What were their priorities and problems?

VIDEO SEGMENT 15

Presenter: B. Davie Napier

Prepare to View Video

Listen for clues to the structure of the Book of Job and three possible interpretations of its meaning. This segment will set the stage for the group's reading of the Job excerpt.

Discuss After Viewing Video

What three interpretations of the meaning of the Book of Job did Napier describe? Which one is most familiar to you?

VIDEO SEGMENT 16

Presenter: Jorge González

Prepare to View Video

Assign each of three listening teams to listen for one of these emphases: the purpose of the writer of Daniel, the message of the Book of Daniel, the characteristics of apocalyptic literature.

Discuss After Viewing Video
Ask the listening teams to report what they heard.

VIDEO SEGMENT 17

Presenter: M. Robert Mulholland, Jr.

Prepare to View Video
Alert persons to listen and watch for information on three topics: ruling powers, religious groups, and the shape of Judaism.

Discuss After Viewing Video
In this period between the testaments, how was the stage set for the coming of Christianity?

VIDEO SEGMENT 18

Presenter: Leander E. Keck

Prepare to View Video
Listen for what is unique about Matthew's Jesus and for what Keck says about repentance.

Discuss After Viewing Video
What is unique about Matthew's picture of Jesus? What is repentance?

VIDEO SEGMENT 19

Presenter: Leander E. Keck

Prepare to View Video
Why does Matthew have Jesus being so critical of the Jewish leadership? Take notes on the reasons.

Discuss After Viewing Video
Why did the early church that influenced Matthew's Gospel feel it necessary to emphasize the tensions between Jesus and the Pharisees?

The group might examine some of the exchanges between Jesus and the Pharisees in order to try to identify the perspective of the early church.

VIDEO SEGMENT 20

Presenter: Dal Joon Won

Prepare to View Video
Listen for reasons the disciples failed to understand the kind of Messiah Jesus was.

Discuss After Viewing Video
Why did the disciples misunderstand who Jesus was? Compare our ability to comprehend who Jesus is and the discipleship he requires of us with that of the disciples.

VIDEO SEGMENT 21

Presenter: Fred B. Craddock

Prepare to View Video
Listen for what Luke wants readers to know about Jesus. Take notes.

Discuss After Viewing Video
Suppose you never heard about Jesus. What did you learn about him from Luke's Gospel?

VIDEO SEGMENT 22

Presenter: Fernando F. Segovia

Prepare to View Video
Listen for what makes John's Gospel different from Matthew, Mark, and Luke.

Discuss After Viewing Video
What are the distinctive characteristics of the Gospel of John? In what sense is Jesus the bringer of life?

VIDEO SEGMENT 23

Presenter: Gail R. O'Day

Prepare to View Video
Listen for and make notes on how Jesus prepares the disciples for his absence.

Discuss After Viewing Video
How are the disciples to be sustained and empowered in Jesus' absence?

VIDEO SEGMENT 24

Presenter: J. Ellsworth Kalas

Prepare to View Video
Listen for two emphases: persons through whom the Holy Spirit worked and the power of the Holy Spirit in their lives.

Discuss After Viewing Video
Which persons did you meet for the first time? What was surprising about this power of the Holy Spirit?

VIDEO SEGMENT 25

Presenter: J. Ellsworth Kalas

Prepare to View Video
Pay particular attention to the strategy followed by the early Christians as they carried out Jesus' command to go into all the world, and to their enlarged understanding of what the world was.

Discuss After Viewing Video

How might we use the strategy of the early Christians in spreading the gospel? If we see the world as more than geographical, how will that affect our ministry?

VIDEO SEGMENT 26

Presenter: Richard B. Hays

Prepare to View Video

Listen for why Paul finds it necessary to answer the question, Can God be trusted?

Discuss After Viewing Video

What points does Paul make in arguing that God can be trusted? Why is it as important to Christians as to Jews to know that God can be trusted?

VIDEO SEGMENT 27

Presenter: Pheme Perkins

Prepare to View Video

Listen for descriptions of the Corinthian congregation and for Paul's two principles.

Discuss After Viewing Video

Who made up the Corinthian congregation? What were Paul's two principles and what ideas did they include?

VIDEO SEGMENT 28

Presenter: Thomas L. Hoyt, Jr.

Prepare to View Video

Listen for the message Paul wanted to get across to the Galatians.

Discuss After Viewing Video

What were the two main problems Paul talks about in Galatians?

VIDEO SEGMENT 29

Presenter: Leander E. Keck

Prepare to View Video

Listen for the purpose and perspective of the Pastoral Epistles.

Discuss After Viewing Video

What was the purpose of these letters to pastors? What was the point of view from which the letters were written?

VIDEO SEGMENT 30

Presenter: William L. Lane

Prepare to View Video

The writer of Hebrews writes to strengthen Christians who are weary in the faith. Listen for what is said about God and the word God speaks.

Discuss After Viewing Video

How is God speaking in our present situation through Scripture and the shared memory of the church?

VIDEO SEGMENT 31

Presenter: William H. Willimon

Prepare to View Video

Invite the viewers to listen for ways baptism symbolizes our set-apartness.

Discuss After Viewing Video

How does baptism set us apart as God's people?

VIDEO SEGMENT 32

Presenter: Jorge González

Prepare to View Video

Assign each of three groups to listen for answers to one of these questions: What was John's message to the seven churches? What kinds of literature are in Revelation? What is the message of Revelation?

Discuss After Viewing Video

Hear and discuss the information groups heard.

VIDEO SEGMENT 33

Presenter: Maxie Dunnam

Prepare to View Video

This segment presents the challenge of discipleship as a means of preparing the group for decisions they will make as individuals and as a group about their ministry following the completion of their study of Disciple.

Discuss After Viewing Video

Invite group members to talk in pairs about the thoughts and feelings they had as they watched this video segment. Then discuss this question: How is every Christian a minister to others?

VIDEO SEGMENT 34

Presenter: David Lowes Watson

Prepare to View Video

The video segment will prepare the group for the Covenant Service. After viewing the video, move into the service without discussion.

DISCIPLE Group Members

Name ______________________________ ______________________________

Phone ______________ Address ______________________________

Name ______________________________ ______________________________

Phone ______________ Address ______________________________

Name ______________________________ ______________________________

Phone ______________ Address ______________________________

Name ______________________________ ______________________________

Phone ______________ Address ______________________________

Name ______________________________ ______________________________

Phone ______________ Address ______________________________

Name ______________________________ ______________________________

Phone ______________ Address ______________________________

Name ______________________________ ______________________________

Phone ______________ Address ______________________________

Name ______________________________ ______________________________

Phone ______________ Address ______________________________

Name ______________________________ ______________________________

Phone ______________ Address ______________________________

Name ______________________________ ______________________________

Phone ______________ Address ______________________________

Name ______________________________ ______________________________

Phone ______________ Address ______________________________

Name ______________________________ ______________________________

Phone ______________ Address ______________________________

Name ______________________________ ______________________________

Phone ______________

Address ______________________________